A Journey

A Journey

MEMOIRS

~

Imru Zelleke

2016

ISBN-13: 9781539891796
ISBN-10: 1539891798

Library of Congress Control Number: 2016918474
CreateSpace Independent Publishing Platform
North Charleston, South Carolina

"We all wish to live. We all seek a world in which men are freed of the burdens of ignorance, poverty, hunger and disease. And we shall all be hard-pressed to escape the deadly rain of nuclear fall-out should catastrophe overtake us. "

Haile Selassie I, Emperor of Ethiopia

"አማራ ነኝ፡ ኢትዮጵያዊ ነኝ።
የሺ ዓመታት ታሪክ ወራሽ ነኝ፡
የሁለት ታላቅ ሃይማኖት ክርስትናና እስላም ባለአደራ ነኝ፡
የሕግ የስርዓት የዳኝነት የአስተዳደር የነጽነት አስከባሪ ነኝ፡
የቋንቋ የፈደል የግእዝ የሰዋስዉ የቅኔ የድርሰት ባለቤት ነኝ፡
የጥበብ የዋዜማ የወግና ዳር የደህሪ ገጽ ምንጭ ነኝ፡
የሰላም ጌታ ይጦር ባለቤት የሃገር አዉታር ነኝ፡
አንጋሽ ነጋሽ ቀዳሽ የሥራአተ መንግሥት ደንጋጊ ነኝ፡
የራሴን ስልጣኔ ያፈራሁ የታሪክ ጥንስስ ነኝ፡
የዜግነታችን ምንጭና መሰረት ይሄ ነው።"
እምሩ ዘለቀ፡ ጥቅምት ፪ሺ፱ ዓ፡ም፡

Table of Contents

Acknowledgements

~

I WOULD LIKE TO EXPRESS my love and endless gratitude to my daughters Adey and Saba for the infinite encouragement, advice and help they have given me throughout the years. These memoirs could not have been written without their moral support and love.

I would like also to express my most sincere thanks to Mr. Ian Campbell who has graciously taken on the task of reviewing this auto-biography. Mr. Campbell is the author of a meticulously researched work, "The Plot to Assassinate Graziani" about the genocidal crimes committed by the Italians during their occupation of Ethiopia 1936-1941.

My heartfelt thanks also go to Jeff Pearce for his support during my writing of this work as well as his gratifying comments on the end result. His book "Prevail" is a precious resource for all students of the Italo-Ethiopian War of 1936.

Due to the Italian invasion, I and many young officials of my generation did not enjoy the advantages of a higher professional education. If we worked and somehow performed tasks far above our knowledge and capabilities, it was thanks to the guidance of our chiefs and mentors in the various government departments where we were employed.

First I would like to express my homage and respects to H.I.M. Emperor Haile Selassie I, who was a visionary leader, a most honorable symbol of our national dignity and historical heritage. In an era marked by a multitude of domestic and international crises in which the very existence of Ethiopia was often at stake, his leadership and guidance inspired old and young alike to accomplish our utmost.

I also wish to express posthumously my thanks and highest respects to Prime Minister H.E. *Ato* Aklilou Habte-Wold who was my chief and mentor at the Foreign Ministry; to H.E. *Tsehafi-Taezaz* Wolde-Giorgis Wolde-Yohannes with whom I served in the Ministry of Interior and who was instrumental in my joining the Foreign Service; and to H.E. *Ato* Makonnen Habte-Wold with whom I worked as Liaison Officer when he was Minister of Information for his most priceless support and counsel during difficult moments of my life. H.E. *Ato* Makonnen was a far-sighted, progressive statesman with the keenest perception of our country's problems and future needs. A lifelong friend and a source of infinite knowledge was H.E. *Lij* Yilma Deressa whose brilliant intellect and sharp-witted humor was legendary and had such a profound influence on me.

Finally, I would like to express my thanks to the United States of America that granted me shelter as a refugee, where I have become a citizen and where I now live in freedom and in peace.

Foreword

~·

A NUMBER OF AUTHORS HAVE described Ethiopia's tumultuous passage through the last century, as that ancient empire emerged from the rule of the legendary Emperor Menelik and his heir apparent *Lij* Iyasu. We have been regaled with stories of how the wily *Ras* Teferi ascended to the throne as Emperor Haile Selassie in 1930 and his attempts to modernize the nation. We have learned about the horrors of the brutal Fascist invasion of 1935-6, the dark years of occupation that followed, the war of liberation, the development of Addis Ababa, and the Emperor's attempts to introduce modern institutions while maintaining an imperial court reminiscent of that of Louis XIV at Versailles. Various writers have chronicled the 'creeping revolution' that brought one of the world's longest royal dynasties to an ignominious end in 1975, the horrors of the 'Red Terror' and the political upheavals and purges that engulfed the nation under 'Comrade' Mengistu Haile-Maryam. And more recently, several accounts have emerged of the war with Eritrea, the conflagration that led to Mengistu's flight into exile, and the formation of the 'developmental state' that we see in Ethiopia today. But for a single author to be able to present this enthralling history in its entirety from the early 20th century to the world of today from his own personal experience is rare indeed.

In this extraordinary and compelling autobiography, Ambassador Imru Zelleke, whose grandfather, one of the founders of Addis Ababa, fought under Emperor Menelik at the Battle of Adwa in 1896, and whose father was a Minister in Haile Selassie's first cabinet, presents what must surely be the ultimate insider's view, bringing history to life with an immediacy that grips the reader.

Having received his primary education first from the renowned Dr 'Charles Martin' Workneh Eshete, then from a private school in Switzerland, his privileged upbringing and the innocence of youth were shattered when the author witnessed the outbreak of the Italian massacre of Addis Ababa of February 1937, and for no reason whatsoever was dragged away together with his mother and little sisters to the notorious Danane concentration camp, that inferno in tropical Somalia where so many blameless Ethiopians breathed their last.

An insider's view this chronicle certainly is, yet the author's reminiscences are punctuated with the balanced, detached view of the internationalist. From the tranquility of early Addis Ababa to the horrors of Danane, from the Peace Conference in Paris of 1946 to the Byzantine Imperial Ethiopian court, from the mass murders of Mengistu's *Derg* to a hair-raising escape to Kenya and on to the rarified world of an international banker, Imru retains an enviable capacity to rise above it all. He has an astonishing memory for the telling detail, accompanied by a philosophical attitude that manifests itself in pithy comments and often humorous reflections that make this autobiography so much more than a mere chronicle.

Perhaps nowhere is this more striking than in Imru's insights and commentary on the personality of Emperor Haile Selassie, who receives very evenhanded treatment, his strengths and weaknesses laid bare by someone who is surely as well qualified to do so as any other living person. The author's accounts of life – and death – under the Fascist regime, with its racism, oppression, mass executions and unlawful detention, are also notably open-minded. Despite having suffered the terrors of Danane as a child (and his brother was interned at the same time in the even more diabolical concentration camp of Nocra), he simply tells us, with only a hint of sarcasm, that the Italians told him he had been "pardoned for his crimes", and has no hesitation in acknowledging that some of the Italians where he subsequently ended up working as a teenager were "generally kind" to him and his colleagues.

Having thus taken the reader on the journey of his life in a remarkably balanced and self-effacing manner, Imru rounds off his reminiscences with some interesting reflections and a powerful denunciation of the Mengistu era. He also has some harsh comments on the political situation that has prevailed since the *Derg*, and some strident words of advice for the young Ethiopians of today. Some readers might take issue with some of his opinions, but this does not detract from the value of the author's insightful account of a long, rich and distinguished life – a life lived to the full.

Anyone with an interest in 20th-century Ethiopian social, cultural or political history is encouraged to read this masterly offering, which will surely take its place as one of the most valuable memoirs to have appeared in recent years.

Ian Campbell, August 2016

Preface

~

ON THE EVE OF NOVEMBER 22, 1974, the sunset was extraordinary and somewhat ominous. The sky was crimson red and the scattered clouds, moving slowly eastwards, looked like burning torches. Wise elders watched the trail the clouds made and read a prophecy in them. Indeed, this sunset seemed to augur ominous times. The pandemonium of the past months had me apprehensive and uncomfortable.

Early the next morning a friend called me and said that many officials had been executed and that I should listen to the radio because there might be some announcements. Twenty minutes later, the Derg announced the summary execution of sixty-two high officials and read out their names. No judicial procedure was involved; it was simply a mass murder. Many of the victims were my relatives and most of them good friends and colleagues whom I had known for years.

The revolution had occurred some months back. The country was in complete turmoil. A military committee composed of low-level and non-commissioned officers had taken over the reins of power and named itself the *Derg* (Council). The Emperor and his government had surrendered all powers peacefully to the revolutionary forces. In spite of this peaceful surrender, the Emperor was dethroned in a most humiliating manner and put in detention. The members of the Imperial family and hundreds of civilian and military officials of all types were arrested and detained. Nobody knew what was going on; the ignorant soldiery of the Derg did not know where they were going; they were advised by some amateur Marxist students who were exalted by the notion of a revolution without any particular objectives other than undefined change. The general notion was to imitate what had happened in Leninist Russia, Mao's China, Cuba and some other countries. However, by the time our new-born Marxist revolutionaries were copycatting the 1917 Russian revolution in Ethiopia, Communism was already dying in Eastern Europe. Instead of bringing a joyful euphoria of hope and zeal to build a new Ethiopia, the revolution opened a can of worms. A friend of mine who later went into exile told me: "Everything we considered bad, ugly and evil has been given free license in our country". Time proved him right, the tragedy of Ethiopia had begun. I will come later to what followed.

Having observed the direction the revolution was taking, I had sensed that at one point it would develop into tragedy. I hadn't been arrested yet, but I was sure that I would be detained sooner or later. So I decided to leave the country. There was no point in going to jail and to an unknown fate. I had sold some of my belongings and moved to the Ghion Hotel. The massacre meant that the time to depart had arrived. In fact, I left just in time, because a few days later, many of my colleagues in the Ministry of Commerce were detained. Thus, a new journey in exile started - one that still lasts. It was during a long and sleepless night in a jail in Kenya that I promised myself to write these memoirs. It took a long time and the passing of many events, but I have at last written them.

Maybe it is too late to start a life-story that spans nine decades. Memory fades, events get blurred, names are forgotten and places become hazy. Softened by the passage of time, events and things lose their edge. I am not writing a history of Ethiopia; it is simply a narration about my life and of the events and conditions through which I have lived. Therefore, I plead *mea culpa* for what is missing, mistaken or misplaced.

Imru Zelleke
Arlington, Virginia, USA 2016

CHAPTER 1

The Early Years

~

I WAS BORN IN 1923 in Addis Ababa, Ethiopia. My father was *Bejirond* Zelleke Agidew. He was educated at Menelik II School and joined government service during the reign of Empress Zewditu and the regency of His Imperial Highness *Ras* Tafari Makonnen. He became a member of the first Ministerial Cabinet of His Imperial Majesty (H.I.M.) Emperor Haile Selassie, in which he served at various times as Minister of Commerce, Finance, and Agriculture and Envoy Extraordinary and Minister Plenipotentiary (EE&MP) to the United Kingdom and the French Republic, as well as Ethiopia's representative to the League of Nations. Having carried out several missions abroad, he was familiar with world affairs. My mother was *Woizero* Azalech Gobena, daughter of *Jantirar* Gobena Goshu and *Woizero* Tsedale Atchamyeleh. After the liberation from the Italian occupation in 1941, she was responsible for Women's Affairs at the Imperial Court until its demise in 1974. According to the Emperor's work schedule, every Tuesday was reserved for women's affairs, when he gave audience to those with appeals and various claims. My mother had an office in the Palace, with some assistants, where they reviewed each case and prepared files for his decision.

I can say that my ancestors from both sides had always served the country and the State in one form or the other. My paternal grandfather, *Negadras* Agidew Imru from Gondar was one of the founders of Addis

Ababa; my paternal grandmother, *Bejirond* Yetemegnu Wolle had once governed the province of Yejju. My mother's father, *Jantirar* Gobena fought in military campaigns with Ras Makonnen, Emperor Haile Selassie's father, and was a district governor in Gondar Province. My siblings were my younger sisters Ketsela and Zena, and from an earlier marriage of my father's, my elder half-sister *Woizero* Mekdes-Work and her brother *Lij* Mesfin. *Woizero* Mekdes-Work was at the time married to *Fitawrari* Makonnen Adefrisew, the son of *Ras* Adefrisew; she is credited with having written the first Ethiopian cookery book. My brother Mesfin graduated from the University of Lausanne in Switzerland, and later graduated in Civil Engineering from the *École Nationale des Ponts et Chaussées* at the University of Montpellier, France.

In the early years, I grew up in a typical large Ethiopian household. What I remember most was that there were many people around, several relatives and a retinue of servants. There was also a continuous stream of friends and visitors who came to see my father for some business or another. There were always a lot of guests at meal times, especially on holidays. We, the children, had our nannies. A monk took care of the spiritual needs of the household, and taught us children to recite the appropriate prayers and psalms until we had memorized and knew by heart the Psalms of David in *Ge'ez*, an ecclesiastical language that we did not understand. He also taught us the Amharic language and grammar, which, by the way, he could not write, so all our learning was oral. Our monk, *Abba* Gabre-Medhin, was a young man whose religious beliefs were almost fanatic. He was strict in his teaching, but otherwise, he was a very kind and generous man. In later years he became the *Gebez* (chief priest and overseer) of Lalibela, where his greatest legacy was to have had all the rock churches painted the color of red brick.

Our compound on Menelik Square in Addis Ababa was very large and contained several buildings. There was the main house that was our residence, as well as my grandparents' large *tukul* (thatch-roofed house) where my grandmother lived, and a big *gibir bet* (dining hall) for large functions. There were several other buildings that housed guests, servant quarters, kitchens, brewing rooms, and storerooms. There were stables for the horses and mules, a garage - for we had an automobile - and a "*motor-bet*" (engine house) for the generator that gave us electric light. It was an adventure for me to run from one place to the other in the compound where something was always happening, and to listen to some braggadocio from the servants whose stories and arguments fascinated me. I remember particularly *Basha* Thomas, who had soldiered with my grandfather at the Battle of Adwa in 1896. He was a short, ferocious-looking man who carried a huge sword all the time. Whether they were true or not, to hear him tell of the great feats he had performed in battle mesmerized me to no end. My imagination soared for hours combating ferocious enemies and hunting dangerous animals.

I especially liked to go to my grandmother's house as she always fed me some delicious food.Her house was a very large *tukul* divided into various rooms with bamboo sticks tied together with colored leather thongs. The ceiling was also made the same way, with a nice pattern to it. My grandmother, *Bejirond* Yetemegnu Wolle, was an extraordinary person in her own right; she held a title usually bestowed only on men. As mentioned, she had at one time been Governor of Yejju province, where she originated from. She was appointed to the post by *Ras* Wolle Betul, brother of Empress Taitu, with whom she was very close. Even these days, such an accomplishment is rare for a woman in Ethiopia. My grandfather, *Negadras* Agidew Imru, came from a Gondarine family of notables. He was a merchant and owned caravans that carried goods from the sea-coast to the interior and vice versa. He was in the retinue of Emperor Menelik when Addis Ababa was founded, and organized the first Customs office. He was appointed *Negadras* by Emperor Menelik, a position that in those days included the governorship of Addis Ababa.

His deputy then was *Fitawrari* Haile-Giorgis, later Prime Minister. My father followed suit years later when he became Minister of Commerce with the title of *Negadras*.

When I was about five years old, my father was sent on several missions abroad and my mother went with him. *Ato* Wolde-Giorgis Wolde-Yohannes, (later *Tsehafi-Taezaz*, Minister of the Pen and Minister of Interior), was his Secretary. His personal secretary, *Ato* Gessesse Retta also traveled with them. My parents were frequently away, but I don't think that I missed them very much, for we were always surrounded by our nannies and relatives. What made a great impact on my life were the illustrated books they brought back with them. They were large illustrated volumes from the Louvre and the British Museum, containing photos of the Pyramids and the many other places they had visited. Although I could neither read nor write in any of the languages, the visual perception of those images opened my mind to a new world. I used to sit for hours gazing at the pictures and listening to my parents talking about their voyages. We also had many foreign friends visiting our house who often brought sweets and biscuits for us children. My imagination was simply fueled by all the stories they recounted, also because my elder half-brother Mesfin Zelleke was already in school in Europe.

~

My real journey into a new life began when my father sent me to Dr. Workneh "Martin" Eshete's house to begin my proper education. I think I was six years old. Dr. Workneh and my father were close cousins from Gondar, and they were also very good friends. Dr. Workneh, also known as *Hakim* Workneh, was a medical doctor, a graduate of Edinburgh University. He was the last physician called upon to treat Emperor Menelik when the sovereign's health had failed beyond any remedy. Dr. Workneh was an exceptional man, and so was his personal history. Captured together with Prince Alemayehu, the son of Emperor Theodros, after the Battle of Magdala and the suicide of the Emperor in 1868, he was taken to England with the Prince, then later was sent to India with General Napier's contingent while the Prince remained at the British Court.

In India, the officers in charge of Workneh could not attend to him properly, so he was lodged with a missionary family, the Martins, who eventually adopted him. He did his schooling in India, graduating as a medical doctor, and served as such in the British Army. As the Indian medical degree did not qualify him for private practice, he went to England and graduated with an MD, and qualified as a surgeon at the University of Edinburgh. He came back to Ethiopia and married *Woizero* Ketsela Tulu, a cousin from my mother's side of the family. He then returned to India and went on to serve as Chief Medical Officer in Burma. Upon his retirement from the British Army, Dr. Workneh repatriated to Ethiopia and was appointed Governor of Chercher province with the title of *Azaj*. Later he became Envoy Extraordinary and Minister Plenipotentiary of Ethiopia to the Court of St. James, the British Royal Court. He was about six feet tall and a very handsome man who excelled in sports. Dr. Workneh's house was in Shola district of Addis Ababa, comprising a very spacious compound with all the compartments of a large Ethiopian household. He and *Woizero* Ketsela had twelve children, of which the elder five were in school in England at the time I went to live with them. The two eldest sons, Beniam and Yosef, graduates from English universities, were later murdered by the Italians during the occupation. The house itself was large, in the form of an 'H.' In the left wing were the living room, bedrooms, and office, in the middle were the dining rooms, and in the right wing were the children's quarters and those of our English teacher.

Thus, my 'hybridization' with other cultures started at a very early age. It was a complete transformation of my life. The family having lived for a long time in India and England, the house was run in the best traditions of an English household with an Anglo-Indian touch. Our mistress was an English lady, and all the family apart from the servants spoke English. All our meals consisted of English dishes. For me, accustomed to Ethiopian dishes such as *shiro, alicha fitfit* and the like, eating porridge, ham and eggs, and boiled potatoes was a complete revelation. Our English governess ran our lives strictly, like in an English boarding school. She was a firm disciplinarian, and so was Dr. Workneh. It did not take me long to learn English. I heard it all day long and it was the only way I could communicate with my cousins, who having grown abroad, all spoke English. Dr. Workneh had a large library of English books, and he received periodicals and magazines such as the *Illustrated London News.* Even if I didn't understand the text at first, the pictures fascinated me.

~

In 1928, my father was appointed Envoy Extraordinary & Minister Plenipotentiary to France and the United Kingdom, and Representative at the League of Nations. We traveled by train from Addis Ababa to Djibouti, and from there by boat to France. The train journey to Djibouti took three days, with overnight stops in Awash and Dire Dawa. It was a colorful journey, and the train stopped for a while at each station. In both Awash and Dire Dawa, there were decent hotels to accommodate passengers. From Djibouti, we embarked on a French ship. I don't remember much of the sea voyage. There was no-one I could talk to on the ship, except for one elderly Englishman who kindly answered the myriad questions I asked. One person I remember vividly was a magician named Gala-Gala, who came on board the ship in Port Said. It was the first time I had ever seen a magician. He enchanted everybody with his humor and his magic tricks. When we arrived in Marseille, we were received by a Mr. Bauvais, who was then the Ethiopian Honorary Consul. In Paris, we stayed at the Legation in Rue Cortembert. *Lij* (later *Ras*) Andargachew Messai was the *Chargé d'Affaires*, and *Ato* Tesfaye Tegegn was First Secretary. At that time, *Ato* (later *Blatten Geta*) Ephrem Tewolde-Medhin was First Secretary in London. We did not stay long in Paris for with my parents, my sister Ketsela and I, plus our nanny *Woizero* Fanaye and the aid *Ato* Alebachew, we were too many for the facilities of the Legation. So the Emperor allowed us to stay in his villa in Vevey, Switzerland, where we moved shortly after our arrival in France.

The villa in Vevey was very large, with a big garden about one-third of which was for fruits and vegetables. I visited the house in January 2012; the present owner has kept it as it was in 1928, apart from the addition of a swimming pool in the garden. There was a gardener called Hans, and we had year-round seasonal flowers, vegetables, and fruits. I remember that the cook, Aunt Clementine, used to make excellent preserves. Mother had brought with her all sorts of Ethiopian spices and ingredients; between her and *Iteye* Fanaye they cooked all kinds of Ethiopian national dishes including teff *injera* (flatbread), and even brewed *tej* (mead). On one occasion, while on their tour of Europe, H.I.H. Crown Prince Asfaw Wossen, H.I.H. Princess TenagneWork and her husband *Ras* Desta Damtew, *Dejazmach* Aberra Kassa and *Dejazmach* Kassahun Hailu came to visit us for a few days, and Mother offered them a full Ethiopian banquet. There were not many Ethiopians in Switzerland at the time, apart from a few students. My brother Mesfin Zelleke, Ashebir Gabre-Hiwot, Leggesse Gabre-Mariam who were at the University of Lausanne, and *Woizero* Senedu Gebru are those that I recall. There were also a few members of the Imperial Guard who came for training with the Oerlikon company on the use of anti-aircraft guns, of which I remember only Captain Alemayehu Filate (later

Dejazmach) whom I frequently saw in the Palace in later years. The son of *Ato* Gebre-Hiwot Baykedagn, a progressive intellectual of the time, Ashebir Gabre-Hiwot's rather provocative political views brought him the disfavor of the Court. He had also written and published a book on Ethiopia which was not well received at Court because it contained a photo of His Majesty at an early age wearing sheepskin, although that was quite a normal thing at the time. Still, after the Liberation in 1941, he was appointed Vice-Minister in the Ministry of Justice; this again did not last long because of his controversial views.

In Vevey, I attended a private school and started to learn French. The school was run by two elderly ladies. We were only about twenty students, most of us foreigners. The school curriculum was flexible and adapted to our age group. It emphasized language, literature, and the arts. The teachers encouraged us to read a lot - a habit that has lasted me all my life, and for which I am still grateful to them. On Sundays, we went to Pastor Flad's house for Bible lessons which were given by one of his daughters who was still alive a few years ago. Pastor Flad and his family had gone to Ethiopia as missionaries during the reign of Emperor Theodros. They had kept their contacts with Ethiopia since that time. There was also Mr. David Hall, with a similar background, although in his case, his mother was an Ethiopian lady from Gondar. He helped Father with many tasks. Occasionally we went to Paris with Father. I remember visiting the 1930 World Fair where for the first time in my life I saw some African art, wild animals and a multitude of other novel things. Whenever we went to Paris, Father usually visited his friend Count Lagarde, who was French Minister in Ethiopia during Emperor Menelik's reign. In recognition of the great services the Count performed for Ethiopia while he was Governor of Djibouti and later as Minister to his Court, the Emperor had bestowed on him the title of Duke of Entoto. When we visited him, he lived in the Palais des Invalides in an apartment for retired high-ranking officers and was attended by an orderly from the French Navy. In later years when I was posted in France, I met Count Arnaud d'Andilly, a nephew of Count Lagarde, and we became good friends, a friendship which opened my life to French society.

Life in Vevey was a whole new experience. Apart from French, I learned to swim and to skate and acquired an everlasting love for reading. We returned to Ethiopia towards the end of 1932. By that time Dr. Workneh had been named Envoy Extraordinary and Minister Plenipotentiary to London. At the end of his mission abroad, my father became Minister of Agriculture. The Director General of the Ministry was *Ato* Takele Wolde-Hawariat, an intelligent and visionary man, and a great patriot, who was later appointed *Dejazmach* and Governor of Addis Ababa after the Liberation.

~⁀

When we returned to Addis Ababa, I went to boarding school at Teferi Makonnen School (TMS). The student body comprised about a hundred or so boarders and about two hundred and fifty day students. In those days French was taught at TMS, and English at Menelik II School. At TMS we were also taught Arabic as a second language. The students who finished at TMS were usually sent to the Lycée Francais in Alexandria, Egypt, and later to France. Those who finished at Menelik II went on to Victoria College in Alexandria, and then to England. The director at TMS was French, and the rest of the teachers were Ethiopians, Syrians and Lebanese. Amongst the Ethiopians, I remember *Blatta* Dawit Oqbegzy, *Ato* Yohannes Redazgy, *Memhir* Ras-Work, *Ato* Kostire, *Ato* Sebhat, *Ato* Sahle-Mariam and several others. The exams for the *Certificat d'études* were held in the French Legation administered by professional staff who came from France for that purpose.

At TMS, the age-group of the students was mixed because some of us had started school at an early age, and others later. It was the Emperor's favorite school, and he used to visit two or three times a week. He was keenly interested in our performance and checked our progress frequently. Since our school diet was not particularly fancy, he sometimes also sent us food from the Palace, particularly on fasting days, which amounted to almost half the time counting Wednesdays, Fridays and all the other prescribed days. The school curriculum was tough, which made it difficult for those students who had started at an advanced age. Eventually, some of the older students joined the Holeta Military Academy. Others who had done very well in school, such as Waqjira Serda (later, Lt-General), Bahru Kaba (later, Colonel), Kifle Nassibou (later, Colonel), Khalid (later, Colonel), Iyasu Mengesha (later, General), Kassa Abraha (later, Colonel), were sent to the military academy of St. Cyr in France, except for Makonnen Deneke (later, General), who was sent to a police academy in Belgium.

Some of the advanced young students gave elementary courses in mathematics and French to the officers of the Imperial Guard who had difficulty understanding their Belgian trainers and the instructions for the new military equipment they were receiving. After school time was over, some thirty students, including myself, used to hold class for these officers. What still amuses me is the diligence and discipline with which these senior people studied. Despite that we were the age of their children, they never gave us any trouble, they took seriously whatever we were teaching, and didn't hesitate to ask us for help. At the end of the course, the Emperor was so pleased that we were called to the Palace, where he complimented us for the good work we had done and gave us each a *Larousse* Dictionary and fifty *birr*. On the dictionaries was embossed in gold, "*Souvenir de Son Altesse Impériale Taffari Makonnen, Prince Héritier d'Éthiopie.*"

Teferi Makonnen School had become the premier school in the country and it being a favorite of the Emperor gave the students a cocky attitude. The Director, Mr. Garicoix, was a Frenchman from the Basque region. The school standards were very high. Students were generally proud and tidy. Spirits were euphoric, and plots and protests of all sorts were always in the works. Sometimes it was about food, other times about schooling and so forth. We also had our odd-balls and our eccentrics. Lemma Mamo was the great comic of the school; he could make fun of anything and everything. Our genius was Assefa Haile-Meskel, who was passionate about chemistry and sciences in general. He went around with a pharmacopeia and had memorized the composition of all sorts of drugs. At one time he claimed to have invented a new laundry soap, and ended up burning some people's clothes, after which he was nick-named "Assefa Science." Whatever the subject of discussion was, he would bring some chemical element into it. I am sure many of the younger generation remember him because he eventually became a teacher. Lemma Mamo, whose family were *balabats* of the Entoto area above Addis Ababa, went on to be a graduate of Holeta Military Academy, and later became a Captain in the Imperial Guard. It is said that one day when the Emperor was taking a stroll in the Palace grounds, he asked Lemma where his family's land was situated, and Lemma answered "right here, Your Majesty" pointing at the Emperor's feet.

The Minister of Education was *Blatten Geta* Sahle-Tsedalu, a friend of my father's. I think he thought of TMS as a hive of troublemakers, for which reason, I suspect, I was transferred as a day student to Haile Selassie I School as soon as it opened. There the teaching was again in French. The Director was a Mr. Malhame, and his deputy was *Ato* Zewdineh Kitaw. Haile Selassie I School was first situated in what was known as *Woizero* Tedeneqyalesh's compound above the Ginfile River, and after the new buildings were finished, it was moved to Kebena, where there is still a school today. During this period, I stayed for a couple of months with my maternal uncle, *Lij* Worku Gobena, in Dire Dawa in the Province of Harar. My uncle, together with Dr. Melaku

Beyene and *Ato* Beshahwured, was one of the first Ethiopian students sent to America where he attended college in Ohio. On his return, he had been appointed Director of the railway in Dire Dawa. There for the first time, I met a Black American sportsman. He had come to Ethiopia as a sports coach. My uncle had invited the gentleman to Dire Dawa to teach basketball to students.

My family also had special ties with Harar province because of my mother's family. My grandfather *Jantirar* Gobena Goshu and his brother *Fitawrari* Alemayehu Goshu had fought together with *Ras* Makonnen, Emperor Haile Selassie's father, in the battle of Adwa and the Harar campaign. Both brothers remained in Harar and made their careers through the ranks. *Fitawrari* Alemayehu later died in the battle of Wal-Wal, the clash with the Italians in December 1934 that created the pretext for the invasion of Ethiopia. Eventually, *Jantirar* Gobena married a niece of *Ras* Makonnen, my grandmother *Woizero* Tsedale Atchamyeleh. Their children - my mother, her sister *Woizero* Mentwab and her brothers *Lij* Worku and *Fitawrari* Haile - were all born in Harar. Because of its easy access to the coast, the multicultural composition of its population, and the railway of which the first section ended in Dire Dawa, there was a very distinct difference of ambiance and character between Harar and Addis Ababa. Hararis felt more progressive and liberal than the rest of the country, which was true in many aspects. The fact that the Emperor was born in Harar also gave them some special distinction.

~

In Addis Ababa, life revolved around the Imperial Court, the power center of the nation and of a polity steeped in age-old traditions and customs. We existed in a medieval era under a typical monarchy, with its accoutrements, protocols, and pageantry. Everything orbited around the Court, the barometer of national life. It embodied age-old canons and values that characterized the nation's body of political and social traditions. Shrouded in a byzantine atmosphere, with its mysteries and intrigues, secrets and myths, it ruled the Empire with a firm governance. The Emperor kept strict control of the government, and all decisions – whether big or small - were made by him. All officials, from the highest to the lowest, had direct access to him and had to report to him regularly whatever was happening in their territories. These arrangements allowed the Crown to be well informed about all sorts of details, which more often than not meant intrusion into individual lives. Marriages in the high ranks were mostly political, made with the approval of the Palace.

There was no lack of saucy scandals in the city, which sometimes caused public merriment. There was the case of a mayor of Addis who, trying to escape from an irate husband, fell onto a pile of red pepper, got caught and received a severe beating. A lyric in a popular song about it went: *"Awoy Kentiba lefuna, lefuna - Quna berbere kamuna, kamuna."* (Translation: "The poor Mayor suffered not only a beating - he also had to swallow a pound of hot pepper!"). Political comments were made with songs and poems, like a comment on the society's superficial behavior: *"Areguande bitcha kalosse - Yezare zemen sew kilisse"* ("People these days are mixed, like green and yellow artificial silk").

On public holidays, the pageantry and parades were really fantastic. The Timket celebration was particularly colorful. Once my father took me to the Timket celebrations in the open field of *Janhoy Meda* (Emperor's field), where the Emperor and his family, the Patriarch, the *Abunas,* church officials and *mequanints* (noblemen) with their retinues were assembled. They were all in full regalia; the ordinary people had washed their traditional clothes with *endod* (African soapberry) which created a bright white contrast to the gold and silver embroidery that decorated the *kaba-lanqa* (capes) worn by the high officials and the gentry. Even the horses and mules were dressed up with finely decorated saddles and bridles embroidered in silver and gold. With the verdant grass field of *Janhoy Meda*, and in the background the emerald green of the Entoto mountains, it was indeed an astonishingly beautiful scene, worthy of a Cecil B. DeMille scenario.

As I recall, the population of Addis Ababa was very small - maybe twenty to thirty thousand - and included a sprinkling of Europeans, Indians and Yemenite merchants and laborers. It extended over a large area, about a seven kilometers' radius from Menelik Square. There were few asphalted roads, the main one running from the railroad station to Arat Kilo via the center known as Arada, and another connecting the old Palace with the new Palace at Sidist Kilo. Otherwise, there were only gravel roads or simply dirt paths. Automobiles and trucks were rare, and their use limited to very short distances; most travel was on horse- or mule-back. Donkeys, mules, and camels were also used to carry goods. The air was clean, and the fragrance of eucalyptus trees was predominant. There were wildflowers and all kinds of bushes, some bearing edible fruits like *koshim*, (abyssinian gooseberry), *kega* (rosa abyssinica), as well as *shola* (sycamore) trees along the streets.

In town, there were very few modern amenities. There were two hotels, the Itegue belonging to the Government, and the Majestic owned by Mr. Papatakis, a Greek citizen married to an Ethiopian lady. The Majestic Hotel was on Haile Selassie *Godana* (Avenue), where the Artistic Printers building stands today. It was burned down when the Italians entered Addis Ababa. There was only one thirty-miles-long gravel road going out of town to Menagesha Mariam, a church built by Emperor Menelik on Mount Menagesha. Electricity was not available apart from a few private houses equipped with generators, and water supply was also limited to a few areas. Greeks and Armenians owned goods shops around town, and Madame Hardy, a friendly, effervescent French lady, ran a high-grade boutique with the most fashionable luxury goods. There was a large sort of emporium owned by the Mohamed Ali family from India, and a multitude of small shops owned by Yemenis selling all sorts of sundries including gasoline. Surprisingly there was also a jazz club where Mr. and Mrs. Ford performed. One day my uncle took me there, and for the first time, I heard jazz music. Mr. Ford was a musician, composer, and a rabbi. Americans of Caribbean origin, he and his wife came to settle in Ethiopia in 1930. After the liberation, Mrs. Ford went on to found a boarding school named after Emperor Haile Selassie's daughter, Princess Zenebe-Work.

A most impressive modern feature was the extensive telephone line network that reached the main cities of the country, which had been built at the time of Emperor Menelik. It appears that after the Battle of Adwa, the Italians agreed to pay fifty million *birr* (Ethiopian currency) in war reparations to Ethiopia. When asked in what form he wanted the payment, Emperor Menelik - the great visionary that he was - asked that they build a telephone network across Ethiopia, extending as far as the borders. Every day the line was reserved for the use of the Emperor until 11:00 am, and was free for public use from 12:00 noon to midnight. Thus the Emperor was kept informed on the state of the Empire on a daily basis. The capital comprised a bustling society that did not lack fabulous scandals and famous courtesans. Few people wore European style clothes and shoes; most wore traditional clothing and open sandals. There were also famous singers and troubadours such as Ferede Golla and Negatwa. *Ato* Yoftahe, the Director of Saint George School, had composed a musical named *Medhine* (Savior) that became famous as presaging the imminent Italian invasion.

Every weekday morning my father - like all the other *mequanints* - went first to the Palace to pay homage to the Emperor and discuss state affairs, then he went to his office. Unless there was a *gibir* (reception) at the Palace, he came back home in the late afternoon. He was always accompanied by a lot of people who had business with him as well as guests and his servants. Then lunch was offered to all in our *aderash* (large hall), on average between fifty and a hundred people every day. To sustain this kind of continuous entertainment our compound was like a small-scale food factory. It was more or less the same in the houses of all high officials. In traditional Ethiopia, monetary wealth was not given high marks. The most respected professions were soldiering-cum-politics, priesthood, and farming. The social scale was divided into three basic categories: the *negash* (royalty), the *angash* (military/civilian), and the *qedash*, (priesthood). Commerce and crafts were for the lower ranks. One gained respect and prestige by one's integrity and fairness in public affairs, the size of one's retinue and household, and by one's generosity in helping and entertaining other people.

For me, the best days were the holidays, Christmas, Easter, Epiphany, the New Year and *Buhe* (celebrating the Transfiguration of Jesus). At Christmas, a hockey game known as *genna* was played everywhere in Ethiopia. It had few rules and no limit of team numbers. The idea was to divide a field in two, hit the ball and bring it to the other end. When the ball is hit high, it is called *kwass abedech* ('the ball went mad'). Every large household and every quarter of the town and every school had its own *genna* team. All young men, children, and even grown-ups used to prepare their *genna* sticks, which were shaped rather like a golf or hockey club. The competition amongst teams was very fierce, and fights flared easily. Coming out of the game fighting like mad and bleeding was considered somehow heroic. Sometimes a group of young people would form a team to go hunting wild animals such as elephants, rhinos, etc. They were regarded as *fano* (hunters), which had a romantic or heroic connotation. On Christmas Eve there was a midnight Mass in all churches that everybody attended. All the other holidays were celebrated as they are today, though maybe with somewhat less pomp, and with a decorum ascribable to the Monarchy.

I also had my nemesis, for suddenly my parents decided that I should be riding horseback instead of the mule I normally rode to school. The news spread quickly amongst the family; my uncles promptly gave me some horses, and I soon ended up being the owner of several horses. *Dejazmach* Mengesha Yilma, an uncle, gave me two beautiful palomino *bora* (blond) horses, which I loved. *Aba* Yimam, who was a sort of general factotum around our house, was put in charge of my training. He was a short, bearded man with enormous energy. However, I am not sure if his method of training was the right one. He always chose – it seemed to me - the wildest horse for me to ride, which gave me the jitters every time. In any event, my horsemanship came to an end with the Italian occupation.

CHAPTER 2

The Italian Occupation

~

SEVERAL MONTHS AFTER I STARTED at the Haile Selassie I School, the news of an Italian invasion became more than a rumor. The first armed clash with the Italians occurred at Wal-Wal on the Ogaden front in December 1934. The commanding officer, *Fitawrari* Alemayehu Goshu, who was my mother's uncle, died in that battle. There was a big wake at our house. He was buried in Jijiga, and my mother went there for the funeral. After this incident, it became clear that war was inevitable. A general mobilization was declared, and in all schools, advanced students were given first-aid training. The head of the training program was a Greek, Colonel Papadopoulos, who had volunteered to help Ethiopia. One day the Emperor came to our school, and we made a demonstration of our training in first aid.

My impressions of those times are rather vague. I was very young, 11 years old, with little understanding of what was going on. However, I remember that in general, the spirit of the people was high, and they didn't think much of the Italian army. There was a lot of boasting, saying that we beat them at Adwa, and we will do it again. Some people were actually lending money to the soldiers to bring them back arms, watches and so forth that they would capture from the Italians. There was an elated excitement in the air, but little did we know what was to come. Except for a couple of thousand men of the Imperial Guard, Ethiopia had no regular army at that time. What we saw were bands of ragtag peasant soldiers, some of them armed but many of them not, rushing to the front by the thousands. Those who owned mules and donkeys loaded their rations onto them; others carried them themselves. Some women accompanied their men to the front. The Imperial Guard went to the front with the Emperor. The cadets from the Holeta Military Academy were sent to Tarma Ber in Showa, to make a second line of defense on the escarpment dominating the Rift Valley.

Meanwhile, the League of Nations had declared an arms embargo which, however, only affected our country; the Italians were permitted to bring anything they wanted through their colonies of Eritrea and Somalia. At any rate, nobody seriously tried to stop Italy from invading Ethiopia. The Laval government in France was cultivating a close collaboration with Mussolini and Hitler and had imposed a strict embargo on any arms destined to Ethiopia through Djibouti, the only access that Ethiopia had to the sea. As a matter of fact, France was the first European government to recognize Italian hegemony over Ethiopia. When the Italian invasion was imminent, some arms were ready to be shipped to Ethiopia from Switzerland. Mr. Bührle, the owner of Oerlikon, the arms manufacturers in Switzerland who was a great supporter of Ethiopia, had them smuggled in the chassis of trucks that were sent to Ethiopia as regular transport vehicles. Mr. Bührle was Ethiopia's Honorary Consul in Switzerland until his death in the 1960s.

My father was then Minister of Agriculture. There was a constant stream of visitors at our house; many of his friends also came to see him because he was not well - his health was failing. There was a lot of debate about the war, which I did not understand, but I could sense a lot of concern in the discussions they were having. It seemed that the news from the war front was not good. It was 1935, the Italians were bombing our troops with poison gas, and they had superior arms in profusion. Some of the high officials were saying that the only hope was some action from the League of Nations and friendly countries. France had betrayed us and closed the port of Djibouti for any transit of arms to Ethiopia, and had seized those that were already at the port. I distinctly remember *Ato* Makonnen Habte-Wold (later Minister of Commerce) making patriotic speeches in Menelik II Square, and *Blatta* Takele Wolde-Hawariat (at the time Director of the Ministry of Agriculture), frequently coming to our house to discuss matters with my father. I remember him particularly because of his forceful gesticulations when he spoke.

Gradually we heard more details from the front. *Dejazmach* Haile Selassie Gugsa had betrayed Ethiopia. He had joined the Italians and had opened the Tigray front to them. He was an important *balabat* from Tigray, being Emperor Yohannes's great-grandson and also the son-in-law of the Emperor, having married Princess Zenebe-Work who had died earlier of some ailment. Some time later we heard of the death of *Ras* Mulugeta, the Minister of War. We also heard of the defeat of his army, followed by the defeat of the armies of *Ras* Kassa Dargue, and *Ras* Imru Haile-Selassie. Colonel Dagne Wodajo and Colonel Belay, both graduates of St.-Cyr, were also defeated or killed in those battles. Shortly after that, news reached us of the final defeat of the Emperor's main army at Maychew, in Tigray on March 31, 1936.

We could see many of the soldiers returning from the front. They were haggard and obviously dispirited. All sorts of rumors were circulating; even we children had become apprehensive and fearful. The Emperor had returned to Addis Abeba. Father was at the Palace all day, and it seemed that discussions were going on about what to do in the future. A decision was made to withdraw to the West and continue the war from there. The whole city was in a panic, afraid of the imminent arrival of the Italians. Then suddenly, the departure of the Emperor for abroad was announced. The day after the Emperor left, my father, *Dejazmach* Wolde-Amanuel and many other high officials also chose exile. I remember it was a Saturday morning when we went to the railway station. Burning and looting had already started, and there was a lot of shooting. The railway station was terribly crowded with people trying to board the train. When we reached Dire Dawa, *Dejazmach* Nassibou Zamanuel (my future father-in-law), who was commander of the Southern front, joined us with some more officials. He didn't look well and was coughing very badly because he had inhaled some poison gas with which the Italians had bombed his troops. My uncles *Lij* Worku Gobena and *Fitawrari* Haile Gobena joined us then. I don't remember much of the journey to Djibouti, except that it was uncomfortably crowded and hot.

~

Having arrived in Djibouti, we all moved into the Ethiopian Consulate because there was nowhere else to go, and in any case, we did not have enough money to pay for the couple of hotels that there were in the town. The consulate was a one-story Indian-style building with verandas all around it. We camped wherever there was space; most of us slept on the floor because there were only a few beds available. Living conditions in Djibouti were simply appalling. The Consul-General, *Lij* Tefera Gabre Mariam and his wife *Woizero* Etzegenet Shiferaw, were trying their very best to assist with whatever meager resources they had. However, they were overwhelmed by the sudden arrival of so many people at one time. There were not enough servants, so we - the young ones - had to serve and help everybody. For the first time I experienced misery and being dispossessed; the impact on the grown-ups must have been terrible. My father's health deteriorated rapidly; he could hardly stand up. I think that it was not only due to the disease, but also the desperation and demoralization caused by the defeat. I don't know what discussions went on between the Emperor and some of the high officials, but after ten days or so, in early

May 1936, the Emperor left Djibouti on a British warship with his family and some close retainers. My mother had asked that he take me with him, but it seems that there was no room for me on the ship. Afterward, some of the remaining officials decided to go into exile in Jerusalem. One person whom I will always remember was Wouhib Pasha, a retired Turkish Army General, who was an adviser to *Dejazmach* Nassibou on the Southern front. He was angry and deeply saddened by the defeat. One day he called together all the young ones. There were Tamrat Yigezu, Kifle Adefresew, Fasil Shiferaw, myself and a few other young men, and he gave us a long lecture on patriotism. He told us that the future liberation of Ethiopia belonged to us, and advised us not to give up our country. It was a moving and exhilarating speech which raised our spirits.

The departure of the Emperor into exile created a lot of disappointment. Some felt that he should have stayed to lead the Resistance, even at the cost of his own life. Some saw it as treason, and others were angry with him for not taking them into exile with him, for having abandoned them to their fate. Given the tragic circumstances of the time, some of the anger was understandable and even justified. My father and some ministers and high officials were disappointed because they were not warned in advance of the Emperor's intentions, particularly since the decision had been made earlier to transfer the seat of government to the West, to Gore in Illubabor, and continue the Resistance from there. Many of the young intellectuals like my brother Mesfin, who had already started the journey to the West to form the Resistance, were very bitter and considered it a betrayal. It was an issue that haunted the history of that time for many years. Although I did not really understand the implications of this act by the Emperor at the time, my sentiments echoed the views of the elders around me, and I especially felt sorry that he didn't take me with him.

However, years later, looking at the issue in retrospect, I believe that exile was the right course, rather than undergoing humiliation and certain death at the hands of the Italians. For the country, his presence in exile turned out to be the banner of Ethiopia's legitimate sovereignty and continued independence, instead of becoming an Italian colony at worst, or a British protectorate at best by the wheeling and dealing conducted by the British after the war. No-one could have represented Ethiopia with such dignity as the Emperor did in front of the League of Nations, where he cut a tragic and historic figure. Neither was there anyone else who had the exceptional personality, the legitimacy, the political and diplomatic skills, and the perseverance that the Emperor possessed, to deal with the extremely precarious position of Ethiopia throughout that period. The Italians had tried everything they could to cajole him, including assuring him of a crown if he surrendered. The British, who still ruled their colonial Empire, had their own vision for Ethiopia, whose independence was an anathema to their colonial policy.

Moreover, looking back further at the Emperor's decision to go into exile, one must also consider the situation that existed in the country after the defeat at Maychew and the collapse of the Ethiopian forces. The people in Raya Azebo in Wollo and Showa had rebelled and were attacking the retreating Ethiopian troops for their arms and possessions. My grandfather, *Jantirar* Gobena Goshu, was shot in the back and killed by some local people during the retreat. A close relative, *Kegnazmach* Habte Mikael, who escorted the Emperor on his retreat from the front, told me that they actually had to fight against rebels all the way, even in Menz district, despite the fact that the people of Menz had close family ties with the Emperor. Furthermore, the Emperor knew that some high-ranking *mequanints* and others were already dealing with the Italians. His most trusted Imperial Guard had been decimated in the battle of Maychew, so who could he trust to conduct a resistance campaign? The country was in utter turmoil. I remember the day after the Emperor left, when we drove to the railway station on our way to Djibouti, looting was going on all over Addis Ababa, houses were burning, and people were shooting at each other. For the first time in my life, I saw dead bodies fallen in the street. Most people did not understand what the invasion would mean for them; some may have even thought that it could be to their advantage. Under such circumstances, I believe that the Emperor took a wise decision in choosing exile to fight another day. Whatever opinions exist about this matter are simply subjective. The fact is that the Emperor played a critical role in securing Ethiopia's independence and national sovereignty in the post-liberation era.

Meanwhile, in Djibouti, my father's health had gone from bad to worse; he was bedridden and could not travel. Under the very difficult circumstances we were in, my mother decided that we should return home so that he could die in his own country. The return journey was uneventful but for the multitude of Italian soldiers, colonial troops from Eritrea, Somalia, and Libya that we could see all along the trip. Arriving in Addis Ababa, we discovered that the *Carabinieri* (regular Italian police), had occupied our compound and made it their headquarters. Fortunately, they had not occupied the main house. In fact, all the furniture and the car were still there. In those early stages of the occupation, the Italians were rather friendly and didn't bother us very much. Needless to say, we also kept a very low profile. About a month after our return, my father died and was buried in St. George Cathedral. It was a large funeral service attended by many people.

I was about twelve years old, and at that age, one's perceptions of events are mostly temporal impressions from what one sees and hears, here and there. They are often fragmented like in a kaleidoscope and become rational only in the case of specific episodes that have marked one's memory profoundly. These were not happy days; an atmosphere of doom permeated the land. In a few months, my mother had lost her father, her husband, her uncle and his son Demissie Alemayehu, her first cousin, and many other relatives and friends. She and the whole household wore black for a long time. The monarchy was obliterated, and the country was defeated and occupied by a foreign enemy. For her and many other families, the whole world had crumbled. For me, the depth and dimensions of the tragedy were not entirely clear, although the death of my father was a tremendous shock because it was the first death of a person so close to me that I had experienced. While my mother was the disciplinarian of the family, Father was more tolerant of our childish pranks. I loved him very much. At the same time, I was distracted by the extreme changes that were happening around us and the country. As I spoke French, it didn't take me long to understand and speak sufficient Italian to converse. The *Carabinieri* in our compound had their own facilities like an auto repair, a carpentry, and even a tailor shop. There was no school, so I used to hang out a lot around the auto-shop because I liked cars and motorcycles. The mechanics fascinated me. I learned a lot about combustion engines, electric wiring, tire pressure and all sorts of things. To the great dismay of my mother, one day I tried to drive our car and smashed it against our gate, which was closed. I had forgotten where the brakes were.

～

As time passed, Italian control over the country was getting stronger. When the Italians entered Addis Ababa on May 5, 1936, they came with something like three thousand heavy trucks, tanks, and other ve-hicles. Eye-witnesses told me that the ground was actually shaking on their passage. Airplanes were flying all over the sky, and armed troops were everywhere. The town had been sacked and some quarters were burning. It was a terrifying experience. Immediately after the occupa-tion, the Italians more or less followed a policy of pacification. Enticed by Italian promises that they could maintain their titles and property, many members of the nobility such as *Ras* Hailu Tekle-Haimanot, *Ras* Seyoum Mengesha, *Ras* Getachew Abate, *Ras* Kebede Ketim, *Afe-Negus* Telahun Habte and other high-ranking officials had surrendered to them. The Italians did not confiscate property, and they paid some rent for the dwellings they occupied. The upkeep of the occupation forces had created huge demands, and the infusion of large expenditures, in turn, transformed the traditional economy into a new dimension. The demands for goods and services had increased enormously. Business was booming, and thousands were employed in menial jobs. All these new activities taken together obfuscated the real intent of the military occupiers and gave a sense of normality to daily life. Deceived by the new prosperity, many people started to collaborate with the occupiers, thinking that they were well intentioned. This apparent calm lasted for some nine months. On February 19, 1937, at a large public meeting held in the Palace by the Italian authorities, two Ethiopian patriots, *Ato* Abraham Deboch and *Ato* Moges Asgedom, made an attempt to kill *Maresciallo* Graziani, who was then the Supreme Commander of all Italian forces occupying our country. This attempt triggered the mass murder and imprisonment of thousands of our people by the Italian invaders.

~

The Graziani incident was a watershed for the Italian occupation, for it revealed the real vicious character of the would-be Fascist colonizers. It gave them the excuse to carry out what was all along on their mind, namely to exterminate the Ethiopian traditional leadership and the intelligentsia who had formal education and military training. These elements were considered dangerous because of their knowledge. In the early days of the occupation, a coordinated attack on the Italian forces in Addis Ababa had been attempted by armed groups led by *Fitawrari* Fikre-Mariam, *Dejazmach* Balcha Aba Nefso, *Dejazmach* Aberra Kassa, *Dejazmach* Asfawossen Kassa, *Ras* Mesfin Sileshi (then Colonel), but it had failed. Under the false promise of peaceful negotiations, the Italians had then assassinated *Dejazmach* Aberra Kassa and his brothers *Dejazmach* Asfawossen Kassa and *Dejazmach* Wondwossen Kassa whom they still suspected of inciting rebellion. Before the departure of the Emperor into exile, as it had been decided to continue the struggle from western Ethiopia, the government had moved to Gore under the leadership of *Ras* Imru Haile Selassie. *Ras* Imru had withdrawn with what remained of his army to the Kaffa region where some leaders, military officers, young members of the intelligentsia and others forces had joined him. Unfortunately, the governor of the region had already surrendered to the Italians, which led to the capture of *Ras* Imru. Thus the planned resistance in the West disbanded. Some people returned to Addis Ababa or went to the provinces of their birth. Groups like those led by *Woizero* Kelem-Work Tiruneh (the wife of *Dejazmach* Amde) and *Dejazmach* Takele Wolde-Hawariat (then Mayor of Addis Ababa) took refuge in Kenya. *Ras* Desta Damtew, the husband of H.I.H Princess Tenagne Work, who was leading the Resistance in the south, was vanquished and killed. Others started to organize guerilla armies in various parts of the country. It was in the midst of all this turmoil that the attempt to kill Graziani was made.

In Ethiopia *Yekatit Asrahulet* (*Yekatit 12*, or February 19, 1937) is celebrated as Martyr's Day, and every year a commemoration ceremony is held on the square by the same name at Sidist Kilo, near Addis Ababa University. When the attempt on Graziani's life took place there were probably more than fifty thousand Italian troops and as many *banda* (colonial troops) as well as the whole hierarchy of high ranking military, civilian officials and a profusion of Italian civilians in Addis Ababa. Graziani was the cruelest and most vicious of the Italian commanders.

He was a die-hard, rabid Fascist, and was considered to be a strict enforcer of the Fascist rule. *Ato* Abraham Deboch and *Ato* Moges Asgedom were intelligent, educated young men. I do not believe that they underestimated the Italian forces, nor that they thought that there would not be any consequences following their action. They simply decided to set an example. In fact, it was their heroic act that revealed the true racist and criminal schemes of the Fascist invasion, and galvanized the Ethiopian resistance and gave it a lasting impulse.

I read in the *Ethiopian Reporter* an article by Bruk Shewareged which related that some people were arguing that the intention of our heroes was to eliminate the Italian leadership with one stroke. Nothing could be further from the truth. Others were saying that they should have considered the pros and cons and the costs and benefits before making the attempt, thereby avoiding the bloodshed. This last argument I find to be a typical reasoning of our times, namely: procrastinate, and wait until somebody else does the job for you, and criticize after the fact. What our two heroes did with their selfless sacrifice, was to show that the mighty enemy could be challenged by a bold and decisive act. I am not a hero, but I give their dues to those who are. Heroes are not calculators and speculators, they are made of pure spirit, they are people who give their life for a good cause, fully conscious of their mortality. Abraham Deboch and Moges Asgedom are pure and authentic Ethiopian heroes who gave impetus and dignity to Ethiopian patriotism at its most critical hour. Their heroism sets an eternal symbol and a noble inspiration for all Ethiopian patriots, especially when our people suffer under the yoke of violent and ruthless dictatorships and national survival is at stake.

My personal recollections of those tragic days are somewhat confused. I hope to be excused if my memory fails me, and for not mentioning thousands of deeds that should be told and a plethora of people that should be remembered. The horror that happened after the attempt on

Graziani's life is unforgettable and probably the most distressing life experience that has marked many of my generation and myself. After the attempt made on his life, Graziani gave free rein to all Italians, military and civilian alike, to kill, beat and arrest any Ethiopian at their whim. There ensued a terrible period of massacre and violence on the whole population. This episode of absolute terror lasted three days. Thousands died and were maimed by the Italians who were using guns, bayonets, knives, even picks and shovels to prey on people, indiscriminately of age and gender. The *Camicie Nere* (Blackshirt Fascists cadres), the *Legione di Lavoro* (Workers Legion) and the *Polizia Coloniale* (Colonial Police) had a field day. Our house overlooked Menelik II Square, and from the second floor, I could see many Italian military, civilians, and policemen killing and beating people who in a panic were trying to take refuge in the Municipality. In my young mind what shook me to the core was the extreme and indiscriminate violence inflicted on peaceful people. Even today after witnessing the unfolding of so many dramas, I find it difficult to rationalize. The massacre occurred all over the country. It is impossible to estimate how many people were killed, some say thirty thousand, but I am sure there were more victims than that.

CHAPTER 3

Life in a Concentration Camp

~

As I NOTED EARLIER, OUR compound in Arada was occupied by and had become the headquarters of the *Carabinieri*. A day after the attempt on Graziani, my mother, my two sisters and I were arrested. I was twelve years old, and my sisters Ketsela and Zena were nine and two years old, respectively. We were kept prisoners in the basement of a villa by our property. We spent a horrible and terrifying first night because there were some Italian prisoners that were being interrogated and were screaming in agony. These Italian nationals were probably anti-Fascists or criminals. The next day they brought us upstairs on the veranda and from there we were transferred to Akaki (in an area known as Nefas Silk) where they had set up a large concentration camp. My half-brother Mesfin Zelleke was also arrested, and we met him in the camp. Hundreds of prisoners were brought there from all over Ethiopia. Many of them were country people and simple farmers; they did not know what was going on and why they were there. The camp was a sort of distribution center from where the prisoners were separated and sent to various prisons and concentration camps.

We were crammed into large military tents with no facilities and slept on the ground with no cover. This was our initiation to the horrid realities that were to follow. Nothing exceptional happened in this camp during our time but for one incident. An Italian sentinel bayoneted and killed a pregnant woman. The woman and her husband were peasants who had never been out of their village and did not understand why they were detained. The woman who wanted to relieve herself, went to the camp gate to ask for directions. It was very dark at night, and when the sentinel saw this big fat woman accost him, he was so scared that he simply impaled her with his bayonet. Her husband, a fellow named Wolde Gabriel, went stark raving mad on the spot, became very violent and was put in chains. He was sent to Danane Concentration Camp, where still chained, raving and screaming around the camp, he died after a few months.

We were kept in the Akaki camp for about a week, then at the beginning of March 1937, they began sending the detainees to the various destinations where they were to be jailed. Some groups were taken to Italy, and a number of intellectuals were sent to Nocra in the Dahlak Islands, the worst prison of all. The bulk of the prisoners was taken to Danane Concentration Camp in Somalia, forty kilometers south of Mogadishu. We were amongst this last group.

∼

If I remember correctly, the journey to Danane took about four weeks. There were hardly any roads - only tracks made by the army during the invasion. The prisoners were crammed into covered trucks without sides, and there were no benches. The trucks were so crowded that no other position but sitting or standing was possible. Prisoners were allowed down from the trucks for a couple of short spells a day to relieve themselves. Otherwise, they had to stay in the trucks all the time. A small amount of food and water was given every day, mostly gallettas (a type of hard bread) and some tomato paste. When we arrived at Dire Dawa, we camped outside the city. By then many people had become sick with malaria, diarrhea, and other ailments. However, a few people who had money on them were allowed to go shopping under guard.

The worst part of the journey was crossing the Ogaden after Jijiga. It was raining heavily, and the ground had simply become a mud pool. Whenever the trucks sank in the mud and could not move, all the prisoners had to climb down and push them. The convoy could travel only a few kilometers a day. Even more people became sick of exhaustion and hunger. Some people died, and as there was no time to bury them, the bodies were left by the road. The Somali *askaris* (colonial troops) who were guarding us were irascible and very cruel; they did not give any help to the prisoners. They would beat a prisoner for any excuse.

Danane was a small village on the coast forty kilometers south of Mogadishu. The prison camp, which was completely erased by the Italians when in the 1950's they were administering Somalia under UN trusteeship, consisted of a very big compound surrounded by eight meters high walls, with guard towers. The compound was divided into four sections one of which contained the administration offices and the infirmary. The other three sections were for prisoners. Inside there were *tukuls* to house the prisoners. However, because of the large numbers of prisoners, open sheds were also built around the walls, where a straw mat and a space of about eighty centimeters was allocated to each person. The walled camp was only for men; the women's camp was outside in a separate area adjacent to the prison walls. The women's compound consisted of some large military tents surrounded by barbed wire. Inside the camps relatives, friends and acquaintances tried to stay together to support each other.

There was no communication between the compounds, but after a while they allowed married men to visit their wives on Sundays. There was no physical contact; they simply talked over the barbed wire fence for the short time that was allowed. Because I was young I was allowed to go and visit my mother and my sisters. At one time I was so sick with malaria that they let me stay with my mother until I recovered. Outside the camps, an isolated tent called Lazaretto served as the last resting place for those who were moribund and could not take care of themselves. They were simply left there to die. A young nurse, sister of *Ato* Bayu Wolde-Giorgis and I were the only ones who went there to give them some water and food. Few of them lasted more than two or three days before they passed away.

I am not sure of the number, but I think there were, according to Italian documents found in later years, some 6,200 prisoners in Danane of which only 3,000 survived. The first few months were terrible. Food consisted of boiled vegetables and *gallettas* that were rotten and full of worms. Drinking water was drawn from wells dug in the vicinity of the sea, which made it salty. In the beginning, there was no medical treatment, although later they assigned a doctor to the camp. People fell sick with malaria, dysentery, scurvy, typhus, tropical sores and all sorts of diseases caused by malnutrition and extremely bad living conditions. Several hundred died during the first few months. On the whole, I think that at least one-half of the prisoners that were taken to Danane died there. Conditions in the main prison were terrible because of the high walls surrounding it; there was not enough air circulation. The hot climate of the area made it suffocating and very unhealthy. There were only eight or ten holes in the latrines, so you can imagine what it was like with hundreds of people suffering from diarrhea.

Every morning the adult males were taken out of the camp to gather wood and do some arduous work that the camp commandant had ordered. In the evening, people prayed and cried '*Igziyooo!*' a group invocation to God. As I couldn't do any heavy manual work because of my age, I was assigned to the infirmary where I helped with cleaning and doing odd jobs. There I saw more death and human agony than for the rest of my whole life. Otherwise, there was not much to do; a lot of time was spent in reading the Bible and some religious literature that was available. Some of the educated took to teaching the young. I learned Italian and many other subjects from them, especially from my brother.

Chess and *gebeta*, played with rudimentary boards, were very popular games. Or else our time was taken up in arguments and speculations about our fate, religions, politics and history that led to endless discussions. There was no attempt to escape because it was feared the people in the surrounding areas were hostile. I heard later, though, that two men did escape and reach home.

On Sundays, we were allowed to go to the beach where we could bathe ourselves and launder our meager clothing. Thank God, the climate was hot and whatever tattered clothes we had were enough to cover ourselves. Some people even became skilled at sewing some garments out of any rags they could find. Occasionally people were allowed to write home, and receive letters from their families. Spirits were generally high; there was always something to laugh or cry about, and people had not lost hope. They believed firmly that they would be free and that the Italian would go away one day. People helped each other in whatever way they could. There were no ethnic divisions; poor or rich, high or low rank, everyone helped everyone. Compassion and generosity are indeed ingrained in the Ethiopian character, and they are particularly manifest in such dire situations. Some of the people I remember are *Fitawrari* Haile Zelleqa, Major Asfaw Ali, Major Bahru Kabba who died in prison, *Ato* Tewodros Mengesha, Lt.-General Iyasu Mengesha, *Fitawrari* Tigre Makonnen Hailemariam, *Ato* Wolde Endeshaw, *Ato* Bekele Tessema, *Woizero* Tsige Mengesha, *Woizero* Atzede Wolde-Amanuel, *Woizero* Shitaye Wolde-Amanuel, *Ato* Bayu Wolde-Giorgis, *Ato* Mokria Makonnen, *Fitawrari* Ambaw Gulilate, *Fitawrari* Wossene Awrariss, *Ato* Tekle-Tsadik Mekuria, and others.

There are countless anecdotes about the Ethiopian moral fiber during the Italian occupation; some are funny, while others are sad. Here are two samples: one tragic-comic, the other heroic: This first story is about a remarkable man. It happened in Addis Ababa's *Tyit-bet* (munitions warehouse that was converted into a prison), where he was detained. Named Dr. Alemwork, he was a veterinary graduate from the UK. The prison authorities had put him in charge of the infirmary. Not only did he not know anything about human ailments, but he also had no medicine to treat even a headache. His only real function was to register the dead in the prison ledger. So in the column that said "Cause of Death," he wrote in Italian, "Morto per la Patria" ('Died for the Country'). When this was discovered and he was interrogated, his reply was that since he didn't know what caused their death, he thought it appropriate to register the real reason for which they were jailed. The Italians authorities were not amused, and they sent him to Nocra prison, where he remained throughout the occupation. The other story is about another hero, named Captain Bezuayehu (later *Dejazmach*). He was a member of the Imperial Guard. In Danane, he used to tell us that as soon as he was freed, he was going to kill a few of the enemy and then join the Resistance, which he did.

CHAPTER 4

Back to Ethiopia and the Resistance

⌒

IN JANUARY 1939, FIFTY-FOUR OF us were returned to Addis Ababa and freed. Then, later that year, another 264 prisoners were released from Danane. By that time, because of his excessive brutality and the spreading of the Ethiopian resistance, Graziani was replaced as Viceroy by the Duke of Aosta. The Italians had reversed their former violent pacification policy and now wanted to show clemency, which I suspect was the reason for our release. My brother was not released; he was transferred to Nocra prison, in the Dahlak Archipelago where he stayed for another year. The remaining "political" prisoners were released from time to time, and those who survived of the original 6,000 or so returned home.

We returned Addis Ababa after another grueling journey across the Ogaden back to the camp in Akaki from where we had departed. A few days later came Cerulli, who was then Vice Governor General, accompanied by Ras Hailu Tekle-Haimanot and Professor (*Negadras*) Afework. He told us that thanks to the clemency of the King, the Duce and everybody in the Fascist firmament, we were pardoned for our crimes. Arriving home, we found the main house and all other buildings in the compound occupied by the Italians and discovered that all our belongings and goods had disappeared. What space was available was only a section of the stables where we had kept mules and horses which had also disappeared. Having heard about our return, a few of the old servants appeared and helped us to clean the place. To call our lodging rudimentary would be putting it mildly, but anyway, it was better than the concentration camp because we could move around and try to pick up our lives. Eventually, we managed to convince the Italians to let us use one of the small houses in the compound, where we lived throughout the remainder of the Occupation. As for me, and those of my generation, we were left in a limbo. There were no schools to go too, and we were too young to get a regular job. Occasionally, a construction company that was building the Bishoftu road hired me as an interpreter for a day or two.

Then Professor Afework, who was a friend of the family, got me a job at the Banco di Roma as a filing clerk. I was fifteen, and a whole new world opened up for me. The work was rather simple, and I quickly learned the filing system of the bank. *Ato* Yohannes Redazgy (my former teacher at Teferi Makonnen School), Alfred Shafi and Gabre Meskel Kiflegzy and another young man called François were already working there. They were very helpful and showed me the ropes. After a little while, I realized that if I could improve my skills I could earn more money. I therefore went to learn some language and typing at a school that a private Italian man was running for *indigeni* (the natives). This training earned me a promotion and better pay, and especially more exposure to the workings of a bank. The Director of the Addis Ababa branch was a *Signor* Bruno, who, together with the older employees of the Bank, was in general kind to us, though a few of the younger ones who were members of the *Fascio* (Fascist Party) didn't like our presence, and were contemptuous. Occasionally they wore their black uniforms with a ridiculous little dagger and went parading at Fascist events.

Meanwhile, the attempted colonization went full steam ahead. Roads were built all over the country, housing developments such as Casa INCIS (the acronym for *Instituto Nationale di Construzioni Immobilio Sociale*) and Casa Popolare were built around the country to house the colonizers, and farming cooperatives such as the one in Holeta were beginning to be settled by Italian farmers. Factories were erected and a huge flux of equipment and goods was imported from Italy. A plan to divide the city of Addis Ababa into white and black sections had been started, and the "Mercato" area had been built to serve as the indigenous market and be the center of the indigenous part of town. Funds were granted to some Ethiopian officials to build residences in the Kolfe area, and these served as pilot projects for a housing development intended for middle-class locals. All this activity generated huge demands on local human and material resources. For the first time, Ethiopia entered into a cash economy. The level of activity together with the introduction of new technologies had a tremendous impact on the traditional social and economic fabric of the country. Ethiopians adapted quickly to the new conditions and started their own business and trading concerns. Most of the commercial activity consisted in supplying goods and services to the occupying forces and to the domestic demand that had increased with the new disposable cash-flow in people's hands. The social pattern had also changed with the inflow of Eritreans, Somalis, and Libyans who came with the Italians as colonial troops and as their retainers. In many ways, the Occupation was a revolution that radically changed a society still anchored in its centuries-old culture and traditional way of life.

My personal life had also transformed; I was in my late teens now and somehow more mature than young people of my age. There was no more family fortune or rank and privileges to bank on; the world in which I had grown up had gone for good. Adulthood came hard and fast. I became a wage-earner, struggling for survival, which instilled in me a strong sense of self-reliance. My social life revolved around my cousins the Workneh family: *Woizeros* Aster, Elsie, Sarah, Rebecca;

Woizero Suzie and her husband *Ato* Mekuria, and other friends like *Lij* Yilma Deressa, who was like an elder brother, as well as *Ato* Befekadu Wolde Mikael, and Marcos Paulos. There was also the *Kentiba* Gebru family: *Woizeros* Senedu, Desta and Yobdar, and Hailu Gebru who was a very close friend. This group was highly educated and well-read; they spoke English, French, and German and were knowledgeable of Western culture and mores. *Lij* Yilma was a graduate of the London School of Economics, *Ato* Befekadu had studied Arts and Theater in Berlin, Marcos Paulos was a graduate in Political Science from the American University in Beirut, and *Ato* Mekuria was an Agricultural Engineer graduate from Italy. My exposure to them was a highly educating experience which benefited me tremendously in those formative years. The Workneh family lived in their house in Shola, and the Gebrus were in the new Mercato area. None of us had a vehicle; we walked everywhere except on the rare occasions when we took a taxi.

We met almost every day. Discussions were always passionate and interesting, ranging widely from politics, art, music, literature, history and science. There were plenty of books, and strangely enough, there was a lot of international literature translated into Italian that we could purchase. We also listened to a lot of jazz music which all the people of our circle were familiar with. A place where all educated Ethiopians gathered - that is, those that had survived after the killing and detentions - was at a café in Mercato owned by *Ato* Tesfaye Kejela, who belonged to the Kejela family, the traditional *balabats* of the Addis Ababa area. He was a jazz musician educated in Belgium, where he had his own band. After the Occupation, he became a businessman. He opened a gas station and a café near Tekle-Haimanot Church which became a meeting place for Ethiopia's foreign-educated elite. Obviously, discussions about politics were guarded. Nevertheless, debates and arguments continued daily about the problems in the country. The notion that we would get rid of the Italians someday had become an act of faith. Some of the people were members of an underground resistance movement known as *Yewust Arbegnoch*, whose existence I only discovered after the Liberation.

~

The guerilla resistance warfare by the Ethiopian Patriots against the Italians had started immediately after the occupation of Addis Ababa, and as mentioned earlier, a coordinated strike to liberate the city had been attempted in the early days. In June 1936, forces led by *Shalaqa* Mesfin Sileshi (later *Ras*) and *Dejazmach* Aberra Kassa and *Dejazmach* Asfawossen Kassa, from the north, *Fitawrari* Fikre-Mariam and Zewdu Abakora from the east, and *Dejazmach* Balcha from the West were to attack the capital jointly. Unfortunately, the attempt failed for lack of communication. *Dejazmach* Balcha committed suicide refusing to surrender, *Fitawrari* Fikre-Mariam, whose forces had penetrated as far as the Church of Yeka Mikael, had to withdraw and died in combat a little later. *Ras* Mesfin, whose forces had reached Gullele, withdrew to Selale and later to Gojjam. The Kassa brothers never made it; they were later executed treacherously by the Italians to whom they had surrendered. Despite all these drawbacks, the resistance warfare did not abate. *Ras* Desta Damtew, fighting in Gurage country, was killed in combat. Among the many other commanders leading Patriot groups harassing the Italians were *Ras* Abebe Aregay in Shewa, *Dejazmach* Geressu Duki in Soddo, *Ras* Hailu Belew, *Dejazmach* Negash Bezabih, and Belay Zelleke in Gojjam. In fact, the massacre committed by Graziani galvanized and strengthened the resistance. Realizing that the resistance was expanding instead of faltering, the Italians had started a campaign of reconciliation and had begun sending some Ethiopians loyal to them as emissaries to the various Patriot leaders such as *Ras* Abebe Aregay and *Dejazmach* Geressu, who, however, did not fall for their ploy; they continued the struggle.

In the meantime, the situation in Europe was approaching a serious crisis. The Fascist voices were getting more and more strident; Hitler and Mussolini were making very aggressive speeches. In Addis Ababa and other towns, the *Fascisti* used to assemble in the Piazza in their black shirts, and clamor for war and the return of Nice, the French Riviera and Corsica to Italy, and Djibouti to the Italian Empire of Oriental Africa (Ethiopia). The Italians had set up radio stations in major town centers of Ethiopia with which they transmitted their propaganda through big loudspeakers installed at the main squares and markets. We did not have radios then; the news came to us through these megaphones. Naturally, nobody believed what they said; we all thought the contrary. While the war was looming in Europe, apprehensive of a growing internal revolt, the Italians were trying hard to pacify the rebellion by promising clemency and all sorts of advantages to the Patriot leaders, of which the most prominent was *Ras* Abebe Aregay in Shewa, close to the capital. His wife, *Imebet-hoy* Konjit Abinet, was captured and brought to Addis Abeba with her two-year-old son Ayele-Work. She was a cousin of the Emperor, a close aunt of my mother, so she stayed with us under house arrest for a while, and escaped later to join her husband in the Resistance.

CHAPTER 5

My Brother Mesfin

~

IN LATE 1939, HAVING BEEN released from prison, my brother Mesfin started a business and asked me to join him, which I did. He managed to buy two small trucks, and we entered the grain trade. We set up two warehouses, one in Addis near Tekle Haimanot Church and one in Wolisso, and started transporting goods destined for that area, and bringing back cereals and grains for the market in Addis. One thing that always impressed me then as it does now is the extraordinary vitality and dynamism of the Addis Ababa market. Hassen Kekia, an Eritrean merchant who made a fortune supplying the Italians forces throughout their invasion, was the first businessman to build the central hub of the new "mercato indigeno" (indigenous market), what is called Mercato now. We also used to call it *Addissu Gebeya* (new market), but somehow "Mercato" prevailed in the vernacular. It grew tremendously in a few months and became the center of all sorts of businesses; everything was bought and sold there, including smuggled goods like American cigarettes. With the opening of new roads around the country and the availability of rapid means of transportation, people traveled back and forth to the capital from all over the country. Residential quarters, small hotels, shops, restaurants, bar and *tej-bets* (tej-shops), tailor shops, barbers, goldsmiths, and countless other businesses opened incessantly. With the increasing demands for goods and services by the Italians, Addis Ababa had become a real 'boom-town.'

Our business went well within the local market, but we were unable to transport as many goods as we wanted. We needed more work than we currently had. At the time the biggest demand in the market was for salt, which the Italians controlled and used as leverage to get the foodstuffs they needed. For any amount of grain supplied to them, one was allowed to purchase a 10% quantity of salt. This arrangement was very profitable, because of the artificial scarcity of salt it created. Again this was a privilege they gave only to certain merchants they favored; otherwise, they would buy from anyone without extending the privilege of getting salt. One day when I had taken a couple of truck loads to the grain storage, which was where the Handicraft School is now, I saw that some of the other merchants were getting more money than I, although the quantities they supplied were much smaller than mine. Puzzled, I asked a driver I knew, what was going on. He told me that if I paid some money to the Italian sergeant who registered our load on the weighing machine, he would let me run the truck around the compound two or three times weighing it each time as a new load. Later the same man told me that if I gave a nice gift to the Major commanding the depot, I could probably get a permit to buy salt. After consulting with my brother, we bought four ounces of gold which we put in a small Ethiopian jewelry box, a *mudayi*, and one evening after work I went to the Major's house, which was where the Wabe Shebelle Hotel is now, and knocked at the door. Fortunately, the Major himself opened the door and asked what I wanted; I said that we were grateful to him for buying our grain and that I had brought him a small gift to express our thanks. He looked at the small box and opened it, looked inside, and put in his pocket. He told me that I was a good young man and that I should work harder, or some words of the kind which I in fact didn't hear well because I was scared and expecting the worst. After that, our business improved. Unfortunately, our good fortune did not last long.

Usually, my brother was the one who went out of town to handle the business while I was doing the work in town. Sometimes he was away for a few days and other times for a week or more. One day, about mid-October 1940, when I came to the office the workers told me that the police was looking for my brother who was in Wolisso and for me. They sounded very worried, and some of them left in a hurry, which made me suspect that something was very wrong. I decided to go and look for my brother. Without telling anyone, I went to an Italian mechanic who took care of our trucks and was a friend and asked him if he could drive me to Wolisso because I had very urgent business there. He was not very happy because it was already afternoon, and there was a lot of talk about rebel activity in that area. Nevertheless, he agreed. When we arrived in Wolisso, I went to our warehouse, which I found closed. When I asked the guard, he told me that the police had been there in search of my brother who had gone to the interior and had not returned for several days. As he couldn't tell me anything more, I asked the Italian friend if he could obtain information from the police, giving them some excuse. When they told him that they suspected my brother of having connections with the Resistance, he made a big scene saying that my brother owed him money, that he was a crook and that he would kill him if he saw him. He was also angry with me for not telling him why I was looking for my brother, which I wouldn't have told him anyway. We returned to Addis at night driving furiously. In truth, he was quite happy and laughing all the way because he did not like the Fascists. I wasn't happy at all; I was wondering how I was going to avoid arrest.

My brother hadn't told me anything, so I went to seek help from a cousin of ours from Gayint, *Ato* Alebatchew Gessesse, who was a close assistant to my father and had traveled with us to Europe. He had become the driver for the head of the Officio Politico, *Commendatore* Franca. I explained to him the problem and that I did not know anything at all. Having known me from childhood and being a close friend of my brother, he believed me. He went to his boss and explained the matter, and asked if he could hire me as an interpreter because I spoke good Italian and French. He also agreed to be my guarantor. Thus I was hired at the Officio Politico as an interpreter. That office handled all local political and administrative matters. At the time there were many educated Ethiopians employed there. I remember *Lij* Yilma Deressa, *Ato* Befekadu Wolde-Mikael, *Ato* Marcos Paulos, *Fitawrari* Kidane-Mariam Haile, and there were others whose names I have forgotten. I think that employing them at the *Ufficio Politico* was a way of keeping an eye on them. There was in fact not much to do, apart from occasionally interpreting for some of the officers.

~

By that time, World War II had started, big battles were being fought in North Africa, and British Forces were attacking the Italians from the Sudan in the North and from Kenya and Somaliland in the South. The meager victory the Italians had gained by occupying Djibouti and British Somaliland was fading into an imminent defeat. And the Ethiopian resistance had increased tremendously. Advance groups were led by *Dejazmach* Kebede Tessema, *Tsehafi-Taezaz* Lorenzo Taezaz, *Ato* Makonnen Desta, and *Ato* Getahun Tessema. The Emperor's forces, with Brigadier Sandford of the British Army as an adviser to the Emperor, were already in Gojjam to coordinate the Patriot forces. Although the Italian radio was claiming fantastic victories with thousands of Allied troops killed, tanks and planes destroyed, the spirit of defeat had already set in. We, of course, were elated. The Italians tried to create an anti-Emperor movement by arming some Ethiopian chiefs who had some grievance against the Emperor. Mamo Hailu, the grandson of *Ras* Hailu Tekle-Haimanot, was given arms and money and sent to Gojjam to raise an army and quell the resistance. He came back not only defeated but also wounded and limping. Mamo had become a friend because before the Italian invasion he had been under house arrest in our house in trust of my father. He was a young man in his twenties, who carried his animosity toward the Emperor as his father did. He believed in certain popular myths, such as, that a bullet could not hit him because he had certain talismans grafted onto his skin. When he came back wounded, I use to tease him about the failure of his talismans, but he took it with grace and laughed about it.

On one occasion, in the absence of the principal translator, I had to interpret for Franca, who was inviting *Dejazmach* Zewde Asfaw, a great-grandson of Emperor Sahle Selassie who had never been in good terms with Emperor, to raise an army against the Emperor's forces. Franca was proposing that the Italians would provide him with arms and money. The *Dejazmach* was very confused. He knew the Emperor would be coming soon, and he didn't know what fate awaited him, so he asked me my opinion in Amharic. Because he had little choice, I advised him to take the arms and money and join the Patriot forces instead. I don't know what he did after that. In the meantime, not knowing what had happened, my brother had returned to Wolisso, and was arrested for the second time and transported back to the Dahlak Island prison. Fortunately, he was freed soon after the British forces beat the Italians and liberated Addis Ababa. Later he told me that he was betrayed by one of his associates in Wolisso and that as a matter of fact, he had been supplying arms and money to *Dejazmach* Geressu's group and other resistance forces in the area, and that was why he had chosen to work on that route.

CHAPTER 6

The Liberation

~

IN 1941, THE MOOD AMONGST Ethiopians became utterly euphoric, for we knew that freedom was near. Seeing the frantic behavior of the Italians, we realized that the British and Ethiopian forces were approaching. One day the British bombed the airport and flew over the city, while the Italians in utter panic hid anywhere they could. The Ethiopians were all out in the open, clapping and shouting victory. We heard later that the Italians were so afraid of the Patriot forces that they sent petrol to the British troops all the way to Awash, so as to speed up their arrival to the capital. Some of the Patriots had already reached Addis Ababa. With their big 'afros,' beards, tattered clothes, bandoliers and guns hanging on their shoulders, they were indeed a scary lot. However, they did not take any revenge against the Italians, because the Emperor had proclaimed an amnesty and had prohibited such acts. The British had delayed the arrival of the Emperor because they wanted to be the first to occupy the city so as to protect the Italians and of course grab whatever property they could find. The day after the British forces entered Addis Ababa, a group of Ethiopians was meeting in a restaurant in the Mercato. They were discussing what to do after the Liberation, when suddenly *Ras* Getachew Abate arrived, sent by the Italians. It is still not clear to me why he accepted such an assignment from the Italians when he knew very well that they were already vanquished and that the Emperor would be arriving in a few days. *Bitwoded* Makonnen Endalkachew and several high-ranking members of the Ethiopian Government had already entered the city with the Allied troops.

In the afternoon of the day of the meeting at the Mercato restaurant, I was with my friend Hailu Gebru. We were strolling around Piazza looking at the British forces, who by that time were all over the city center. Hailu had heard about the meeting and wanted to go there. I declined because it was late afternoon and I was afraid that my mother and the family would worry about me. However, my friend went on his ill-fated journey. From what I heard, there was a great deal of heated debate and excitement when *Ras* Getachew arrived. It seems that he wanted to disband the meeting, but nobody wanted to listen to whatever he had to say, and he left shortly afterward. Meanwhile, the restaurant had been surrounded by Italian security forces who opened fire and gunned down the people inside. Many were wounded, and unfortunately for him, my friend Hailu's wounds were fatal. As soon as I heard of the incident, I rushed to the Lambie Hospital (now the Pasteur Institute), but unfortunately, it was too late. The doctors told me that he had been virtually cut in half by machine-gun bullets. Hailu Gebru was the son of *Kentiba* Gebru Desta. He was a very intelligent, witty and charming young man, like many members of that family. He had been educated in English and was assigned as an interpreter for English-speaking foreign correspondents during the Italian invasion. His brother, Meshesha Gebru, an officer in the Ethiopian Army, was assassinated by the Italians after the Graziani incident, together with many Ethiopian dignitaries and members of the armed forces like Major Kifle Nassibou, a graduate of St.-Cyr Military Academy and the son of *Dejazmach* Nassibou Zamanuel, Commander of the Southern Front, himself a victim of Italian poison gas. The profound tragedy of Hailu's murder is that it happened the day that Ethiopia – the country he loved so much - was liberated and that he didn't have the chance to serve and enjoy his country as so many of us did. For his family and all of his friends, our first day of liberation started sadly with the heartbreaking loss and funeral of a wonderful brother.

⁓

It did not take long for the British forces, which were composed largely of South African and colonial contingents, to impose their apartheid policy. As soon as they occupied Addis Ababa and the main towns, signs appeared in public places like hotels, restaurants cinemas, and other facilities that these were for "Whites Only." After five years of Italian brutal racism, Ethiopians did not take kindly this kind of affront. They tore down the signs wherever they were, and fought the British who tried to impose them. It appears that some killings occurred, after which the British withdrew their apartheid signs. Moreover, the British were creating all sorts of difficulties to prevent the Ethiopian Government from organizing and functioning properly.

At that time, I had been sent to Harar to work as private secretary to the Duke of Harar, H.I.H. Prince Makonnen Haile Selassie. As soon as he started forming the government, the Emperor had sent the Duke together with a strong representation to Harar to take over the administration of the province. The group consisted of *Ras* Andargachew Messai, Deputy Governor; *Dejazmach* Letibelu Gebre, advisor; Dr. Ambaye Wolde Mariam, Political Adviser; *Ato* Menasse Lemma, Secretary General; *Kegnazmach* Haile Makonnen, Governor of Harar and surroundings; Lt.-General Merid Mengesha, Governor of Dire Dawa; *Dejazmach* Kifle Dadi, Governor of Chercher; and Major Tamrat Zegeye, *Aide de Camp* to the Duke.

In Harar and Dire Dawa, the British forces were creating as many difficulties as possible to frustrate the establishment of our government. They had occupied all the principal buildings and gave us only three or four houses in Harar and the same in Dire Dawa. No Ethiopians were allowed to carry arms in the cities. The British were also looting and carrying away all the movable Italian property and equipment they could lay their hands on while evacuating all the Italians and their families. In fact, we had to hide some Italians, most of whom were technicians we could make good use of, who did not want to be sent away as war prisoners of the British. Having unilaterally reinstated the colonial status of Eritrea and Somalia under a British military administration, some elements in the British Colonial Office were advocating the breaking-up of Ethiopia on an ethnic basis. Our government in those early days had very limited financial and material resources to confront another military occupation and such adverse policies by the very forces that had helped to liberate the country. To the credit of the Emperor and his team, a highly skilled and strenuous political and diplomatic struggle was conducted successfully against these attempts on our sovereignty. Nevertheless, the British were able to impose their occupation of the Ogaden as a "reserved area" for a period of ten years.

As for me, I settled well in Harar. The Duke of Harar was a bright, most gentle and generous patron who treated me as a brother. An important mission entrusted to the Duke was to establish contact with the people in Eritrea, so in mid-September 1941 we journeyed to Asmara. Accompanying the Duke were *Dejazmach* Letibelu Gebre, two Eritreans Dr. Ambaye Wolde Mariam and Colonel Kassa Abraha, and my uncle, *Fitawrari* Haile Gobena. The British authorities did not approve of the mission and did nothing to facilitate the trip. In fact, we were stopped at a military checkpoint in Kombolcha, a few kilometers before Dessie, and asked to identify ourselves. Unfortunately, nobody had thought of bringing identification papers; the only evidence we had was the Duke's army cap with a General's insignia. When the Duke explained that he was a General and the son of the Emperor, the officer in command of the post wouldn't believe him, and wanted to check with his superiors. We heard him loudly saying, "There is a kid here who claims to be a General and a son of the Emperor. He also says that he is the younger brother of the Crown Prince who is in Dessie. What should I do with him?" Things were eventually sorted out, and our two-car convoy was escorted under armed guard and delivered to the Crown Prince's residence in Dessie. By the time we arrived in Asmara, the British officials there had been informed of the Duke's visit and had arranged rooms for the mission in the CIAO hotel, which was reserved for Italian officers only. We stayed three days in Asmara, during which time the Duke received and entertained many local dignitaries, church and community leaders, most of whom wanted Eritrea to reunite with the Motherland. It was a highly emotional, memorable and historic encounter for both the mission and the people of Eritrea. Thus began the first official *démarche* by our government towards the reunification of Eritrea.

Mission accomplished, we returned to Harar. Because of the various restrictions that the British military administration had imposed, our functions there were rather limited to local affairs that could be handled by the provincial administration. The presence of the Duke in Harar was mainly a political act to confirm our sovereignty over the territory. The British were trying to pry the Ogaden away from Ethiopia under the guise of a "reserved area" where they could station troops in case the war in the Far East extended itself to East Africa. This attempt was, in fact, a flimsy excuse to cover up British wider colonial intentions to create a 'Greater Somalia' under their protection. They also instigated an armed rebellion by some local insurgents whose forces were aiming to occupy Harar. At the time we had no military units in Harar, and the rebel elements were drawing close to the town. Hence it was decided that the Duke should return to Addis Ababa. Meanwhile, the rebels were held back momentarily by some irregular troops led by *Dejazmach* Berhane-Maskel Wolde-Selassie (then a Colonel). Shortly after that, Patriot Forces led by *Ras* Abebe Aregay proceeded to Harar, and they quelled the rebellion. This action was also meant as a direct demonstration to the British military authorities that they couldn't do as they wanted and that we would challenge, if necessary by force, any sedition they were fomenting in the country. Moreover, the British were conniving to separate western Ethiopia and create another division of the country. With all the pressure that the British were exerting, our government wisely conceded to the occupation of the Ogaden as a "reserved area" for ten years. I believe that this concession somehow eased British pressure. Also, the war in North Africa was going badly for the Allies, which forced the British to move their army out of Ethiopia to the North African theater.

~

My life in Harar was very pleasant, and the workload was not too much. However, over time I became restless; the sedate provincial life was not for me. I wanted to be in Addis Ababa, where everything was happening, and where all my family and friends were living. So one day I took leave from the Duke and went back to Addis Ababa, without saying when I would return. After a couple of weeks, I decided to start a business of my own and went to the Ministry of Commerce to get a license. In those days, apart from the Ministries of Defense and Interior, all the ministries were situated in the Palace compound. I was waiting to see some official, when there suddenly appeared *Ras* Andargachew Messai (then *Afe-Mesfin* and Deputy Governor of Harar) with two Imperial Guard soldiers who arrested me for dereliction of duty for abandoning my post without permission. To my great embarrassment, I was escorted under guard across the Palace grounds with everybody wondering what was going on and speculating about my fate. Then I was put in a small room in one of the small villas in the grounds. A couple of hours later, *Ras* Andargachew came and said that I was to return immediately with him to Harar. I went back without even taking my toothbrush. In Harar, the Duke, who was always gentle, asked me why I had wanted to go back to Addis Ababa. I told him that I wanted to start a business. He laughed about it, and that was the end of the matter.

In Addis Ababa, there were many social circles, ranging from conservatives, patriots, military, former exiles, intellectuals, merchants, family and regional groups. Because of family relations and personal connections, I frequented many of them, including *Hakim* Workneh and his family, my elder sister *Woizero* Mekdes-Work Zelleke, and my elder brother *Lij* Mesfin Zelleke. I also visited *Tsehafi-Taezaz* Wolde-Giorgis and *Ato* Aklilou Habte-Wold who was a school friend of my brother. In those days many people educated in France gathered at *Ato* Aklilou's house, where I used to go with my brother, and where I made friends with the Habte-Wold family. Occasionally *Tsehafi-Taezaz* Wolde-Giorgis, who had been on missions to Europe with my father, and *Ato* Makonnen Habte-Wold, were also present. They were very friendly gatherings; the conversation was always lively and interesting. *Ato* Makonnen Habte-Wold was also a friend of my late father.

The post-liberation mood was jubilant and highly motivated towards building the nation. People were doing their best and working with fervor at whatever task they were doing. However, a consolidation of various power centers was also underway. On the one side was the so-called Exiles group that had returned with the Emperor, and on the other side were the Patriot forces who had remained in the country and conducted the resistance against the Italians. In between these major factions, there were other smaller groups with their own interests. Generally speaking, the ministerial cabinet was dominated by the 'Exiles' group, and the provincial administration was left to the Patriots. Personally, my politics were not yet defined, and neither did I clearly understand the power struggle that was going on. My concern at the time, like most of my contemporaries, was mainly to earn a living and serve the country. We were all infused with burning patriotism.

After a couple of months more in Harar, I went back to Addis Ababa with the Duke. I visited *Lij* Yilma Deressa, who had married to my cousin *Woizero* Elsie Workneh, daughter of *Hakim* Workneh. He was then Director-General of the Ministry of Finance which he was organizing. Having heard that I was looking for work, he hired me. I was assigned to the Tobacco Monopoly that was being newly set up. In charge was a Georges Lucas, a Frenchman of Hungarian origin who was a school-mate of Prime Minister Aklilou Habte-Wold. A lawyer by profession, Lucas drafted the laws regulating the Monopoly and organized its administration. I guess I was assigned to work with him because I spoke French. For me, it was a novel experience, from which I learned something about the cigarette business. I also had the opportunity to go around the country setting up distribution centers and sale outlets. Just after the Liberation, there was a lot of contraband coming through Djibouti, Somaliland and Eritrea that was very difficult to control. The British-American Tobacco Company was our principal supplier of cigarettes and tobacco products, and they remained so for many years. Ironically, they were also the main suppliers to the contraband trade through Aden and Djibouti markets.

CHAPTER 7

The Imperial Court

~

THE IMPERIAL COURT HAD ITS traditional well-defined structure and organization. The Emperor kept such a tight control over the government that it was a case of micro-management at its extreme, often affecting people's personal lives beyond public affairs. There was also a network of intelligence and freelance informers, seeking favors in one form or another. It was a byzantine Court with all the attendant secrets, myths, and obscure intrigues. The Court's protocol was rigid and rigorously kept, with its specific anomalies where precedence and power did not necessarily follow rank. All powers were centered in the Emperor and every aspect of national life revolved around the Court including the legal system since the Emperor was the Supreme Justice of the Land. The reader will find that *"Zikre Neger"* ("Imperial Records") by *Balambaras* Mahteme-Selassie Wolde-Maskal, describes the Imperial Court in detail. The most interesting aspect of the Court was the conduct of its politics, which was a highly sophisticated process of balancing multiple interests and tendencies while maintaining the supremacy and centrality of the Imperial Crown. Both Emperors Menelik and Haile-Selassie excelled in this art, which required a tremendous aplomb, perspicacity, vision and rigorous personal discipline - qualities rarely possessed by most people unless given an inborn proclivity coupled with pronounced ambition and ruthlessness.

Traditionally, the Ethiopian monarchy was very close to the people with whom it shared a day-to-day life such as daily *gibir* (repast), in which everybody who happened to be at the Palace that day participated according to rank and status. Then there was the *Chilot* - the Imperial Court of Justice – where state affairs and private claims of one sort or the other were heard and decided upon. It was an open tribunal, presided by the Emperor himself, to which any Ethiopian had the right to appeal for a final decision on whatever judicial issue. It was also an open forum sensitive to the "vox populi" where any citizen present could express his opinion. It is said that Emperor Menelik always asked *"Hizbu min ale?"* ("What did the people say?"), because he felt uncomfortable when the people were silent. From the early years of his reign until the Italian invasion, Emperor Haile Selassie followed the same practice and continued doing so up until the end of his reign. However, by then, Ethiopia had changed; a modern governing system had come into being. This was partly because the Italians had introduced new administrative systems and structures, and partly due to the British insistence on the modernization of the judicial system, the army, the police and the finances, and finally because the State itself needed to acquire international status and recognition.

The Emperor tried to reconcile the two practices; he was a very hard worker. His days were highly organized. In the morning from 9:00 am to noon he gave audience to the Ministers and other officials, and at noon he presided over the *Chilot* which gave final judgments. In the afternoon he visited hospitals and other institutions, then from 6:00 to 8:00 pm he received more officials and dealt with state affairs. He dedicated one day a week to review and consider appeals and petitions presented by women. He attended all church and state functions. All this worked very well in the early days when the government was small and manageable.

To return to the subject of the Imperial Court, what was fascinating about it was its secretiveness and opacity. There are two ways of looking at the Court: one from the inside, and the other from the outside. There were hundreds of people employed in the Palace, from the Minister of the Court down to the stable-boys. Most people had a distinct function, but there were also some with no specific role. Depending on their duties, some were close confidants to the Emperor and the Imperial family. However, one immutable rule was absolute secrecy about whatever happened in the Court. All this produced a state of mind that rippled through the ranks and created an inscrutable aura of mystery. Whether they knew any secrets or not, this secretiveness was perpetuated by all courtesans and employees alike. Even those who actually knew little or nothing could assume an air of importance. Thus for the outsider, the Imperial Court projected an awesome image of power.

There were also practices of the court that enhanced its obscure, enigmatic ways and kept people on their toes. For example, appointments to state office were generally made on national holidays. Suddenly there were rumors that big appointments were to be made. Then followed all sorts of speculations about who was to be demoted or promoted. As a matter of fact, the exercise was known as "*shum-shir*" (promotion-demotion). People started scurrying around, some in panic in fear of losing their position, others hoping to get a promotion. Real pandemonium came about with every expanding gossip. All sorts of people were consulted - wives, parents, relatives - even house servants of the Palace. The whole town was full of expectations. Then, to the dismay of all, nothing happened. At other times, certain people were suddenly called to the Palace, when you got there you saw that others are also gathered. Everybody suspected that there would be nominations. Nobody talked about it, but there would be a strong sense that something important was about to happen. We would all stand on the veranda by His Majesty's office, time would pass, and anxiety would grow with each person ruminating about his fate. After a while, we were called one by one to the Prime Minister's office and told of our appointment. This was the moment when you could accept or refuse the appointment. Refusal was exceptionally rare; if you were unhappy, you accepted and complained later. On the whole, the general environment around the Palace can best be described as Kafkaesque.

As time went by and as the country started to develop and the government grew incrementally, the distance between the Emperor and the people widened further. Instead of trying to pursue the type of micro-management to which the Emperor accustomed, what he should have done was to delegate more power to the executive bodies, and himself keep his traditional close touch with the people and their needs. As Ethiopia's role in international affairs increased and his extensive travels abroad took more and more of his time, while the increasing exigencies of multiplying domestic affairs required more attention than ever, the old system became incongruous. Unfortunately, the lack of delegating power to the administrative bodies served also to diffuse responsibilities and provided a good excuse for inefficiency and procrastination by the bureaucracy.

CHAPTER 8

Ministries of Interior and Foreign Affairs

~

ONE DAY IN EARLY 1942, I went to the Palace to pay the usual courtesy to the Emperor. It was an absolute practice that everybody had to do, to show one's loyalty and respect. After I had bowed and paid my courtesy, I hung around in the garden that surrounded the Emperor's office. It was a sort of open-air waiting room. Ministers and high officials stood there waiting for an audience. There were also many idle members of the establishment who attended the Court waiting for an appointment or some other grant. It was the ideal gathering place to hear all the gossip and rumors about what was going on in the Government or in the Palace, which was the same thing anyway. One day while I was standing there listening to the chatter, I was called to the Emperor's office. There was only *Tsehafi-Taezaz* Wolde-Giorgis present. The Emperor told me that I was to work at the Ministry of Interior from then on and that *Tsehafi-Taezaz*, who was then Minister of Interior, would assign me my duties. He also warned me that if the Minister did not approve of me, it would be the end of my career in government. I guess that the warning was somehow for both of us - for me to behave myself and work hard, and for the Minister not to do me any favors because of my family ties with the Emperor. As the Minister had a reputation of being a difficult man to work with, the warning left me with a lot of apprehensions.

The next day early in the morning, I went to the Minister's office and awaited his arrival. When he arrived, I greeted him, but he pretended not to see me and went into his office and called some other people in. This went on every day for over a month. Then one day the Minister stopped by me and asked me sarcastically "When will you have time to see me?" That meant trouble for me, so I decided to face him right there and then and said: "Now would be a convenient time!". So he invited me to his office. He sat behind his desk and asked me what I wanted. I bluntly answered that I did not want anything but for the Emperor's order to work at the Ministry, and continued by saying that I was sad and disappointed with him. I said "You are a most important Minister of the Empire and I am a small young man looking for a job. How dare you speak to me like this? Why don't you simply say that you don't want me at the Ministry? Anyway, I did not ask to come here nor do I want to work here." After this outburst, I thought that he would kick me out of his office instead, to my surprise, he smiled and told me that I was assigned as Secretary to the Health Department, which was part of the Ministry of Interior in those early days.

Tsehafi-Taezaz Wolde-Giorgis Wolde-Yohannes was a brilliant and hard-working politician. He was a strong and generous man, extremely loyal to his friends and a mortal enemy to his opponents. He was temperamental and very sensitive about his position and did not lend himself well to criticism. He did not tolerate incompetence and sloppiness and did not mince his words about it. Besides being Minister of the Interior, he was also Minister of the Pen (hence his title, *Tsehafi-Taezaz)*, which could be equaled to being the CEO of the Empire. Since all decisions and appointments by the Emperor went through him for execution, he had tremendous power and responsibility. Obviously, this did not buy him many friends amongst those competing for power and imperial favors. His albatross was his brother, *Ato* Makonnen Wolde-Yohannes, who was in charge of Enemy Properties, and whose uncouth behavior and arrogance antagonized many people.

At that time the body-politic was divided into three main factions: a) The former Exiles group, b) the Patriots group, and c) the nobility or the old established class. As there is no hereditary aristocracy in Ethiopia, the latter was somehow spread between the other two, without any common stand of its own. I must say that, at the time, my politics were rather elementary and mainly consisted of a lot of patriotic euphoria. I did not understand clearly the power play that was going on, and I also had my own problems. On one side there was my brother Mesfin Zelleke whom I loved very much and respected, who had criticized the government for asking for British help in quelling the Woyane unrest in Tigray in 1943 and using British planes to bomb the rebels. He was arrested and jailed for a while, which made him one of the first political prisoners after the Liberation. In fact, he never joined any government service. On the other side was my mother who was a cousin of the Emperor and extremely loyal to him. Moreover, my mother and my half-siblings had quarreled over some insignificant inheritance - a quarrel exacerbated by personal incompatibility - and had gone to court. I loved all of them, which put me in the middle. Another issue was that my half-sister *Woizero* Mekdes-Work Zelleke had married *Ato* Ashebir Gabre-Hiwot, who was in disfavor at Court because, as I mentioned, of the Emperor's photograph dressed as a barefoot sheepskin-clad shepherd boy that appeared in his book. Another issue that earned him disapproval was that, before the Italian invasion, *Ato* Ashebir had on his return to Ethiopia married a certain *Woizero* Aster, a famous lady at the royal Court who had been the subject of some scandal. Faced with this dilemma with one part of the family loyal to and in good standing with the Crown and the other in disfavor, I decided to avoid the matter by simply not getting involved and pursuing my career. The whole chicanery put me off; I never had much interest in land or money anyway.

At that time, the Head of the Health Department was *Lij* Araya Abebe. Before him, it had been a Colonel MacLean, a British MD. The British Military Administration had kept the department as it was during the Italian administration. It was a large department employing more than twelve hundred people in hospitals, clinics, a central medical store, leprosaria, mental hospitals, a medical laboratory and so forth. Many Italian medical doctors and other staff had remained in place. Because of the war, there was a shortage of medicines and medical equipment. There were no Ethiopian medical doctors then, only some trained nurses. As Secretary my duties were not difficult, it was just a matter of continuing the existing routine. Besides, some of the elder people who had been in the department longer than I were kind enough to coach me. Shortly after that, Dr. Campbell, an American medical doctor, was hired to run the department which badly needed professional guidance. I got along very well with Dr. Campbell, and as I spoke English we communicated easily. He was a very kind man. When he realized that I spoke fluently French and Italian as well, he advised me to try to join the Foreign Service, where he thought I would be more useful. In fact, I suspect that he might have mentioned it to *Tsehafi-Taezaz* Wolde-Giorgis, because soon after, in 1944, I was transferred to the Ministry of Foreign Affairs.

My time at the Ministry of Interior had been very edifying because I participated in other works of the Ministry as well. The Vice-Minister of Interior was *Ato* Alemayehu Tena, and the Director-General was Major Yohannes Abdu. At one point a committee of departmental heads was set up to draft an administrative manual for the Ministry of Interior. I represented the Department of Health. We conducted extensive research, reviewing many British, French and Italian manuals, as well as our own traditional governance system. Eventually, we presented a manual which was adopted by the government and remained in place for many years. For me, it was an eye-opener on many aspects of administrative functions and methods of governance - particularly regarding the administration of the Interior because the approach attempted to reconcile the new modern system with the traditional practice to which the newly appointed governors were accustomed. Most of the new provincial administrators were elderly notables or former patriot leaders; they had little experience in the new methods and all the new bureaucratic procedures involved.

~⁓

When I was transferred to the Ministry of Foreign Affairs in 1944, I joined the Minister's private Secretariat with *Ato* Menda and *Ato* Demissie. *Ato* Menda and I shared the duties of the Secretariat, and *Ato* Demissie was responsible for the secret archives. *Ato* Aklilou was then Vice-Minister, *Ato* Gashaw Zelleke was Director-General, *Ato* Yilma Gebre-Kidan Secretary-General, *Ato* Tewelde-Berhan a departmental head, and *Ato* Berhanu Tessema Chief of Protocol. Mr. John Spencer was Adviser. The main issues at the time were the negotiations of the Anglo-Ethiopian Treaty of 1944, preparations for the meeting to establish the United Nations Organization to be held in San Francisco in 1945, and later in the same year the First General Assembly of the Organization in London, and the Peace Conference in Paris in 1946. All these preparations involved a huge amount of work to be accomplished, all in a critical situation aggravated by a grave scarcity of resources across the board.

The initial few years just after the Liberation were very difficult times for the government. There was a very serious shortage of trained personnel, no money, and no equipment. The British forces had taken away everything that was movable upon the departure of the Italians - even the furniture. Moreover, several internal crises had developed. In a hurry to move their forces to North Africa, the British insisted that Ethiopian forces should take the principal role in the liberation of Gondar, with British air support. Thus Patriot forces were diverted to that campaign. Soon afterward an uprising, encouraged by the British, occurred in the Ogaden, and rebel forces advanced close to Harar, which again required the intervention of Patriot forces. Then the Woyane uprising occurred in Tigray, for which a large contingent of armed forces had to be sent to quash it. While all this was going on, both central and provincial administration were being organized and borders were secured. Taxes and revenue collection also had to be established, regular Armed Forces and Police had to be formed and trained, and many state functions had to be instituted and made to work.

The British officials, whose background was in their colonial administration, created as many stumbling blocks as possible. Although our sovereignty was recognized and we were members of the Allied nations, some of these officials wanted to impose a sort of protectorate over Ethiopia. It is in the midst of all these activities that foreign policy was formulated, and the political and documentary framework for our claims for reparations from Italy and the reintegration of Eritrea with the Motherland was prepared. Indeed, this was a very intense period of activity, and how all this was achieved in such a short time is still a mystery to me. Maybe it was the extraordinary spirit of patriotism and enthusiasm the people had that prompted them to outperform themselves. For my part, most of my time was spent ciphering and deciphering endless coded messages from Embassies and other sources. Incidentally, I learned a lot from all this activity.

1. Family: from left to right, my sister Mekdes-Work Zelleke,
my Father Bejirond Zelleke, my mother Woizero Azaletch
Gobena, myself as a toddler, an aunt, Woizero Kelemwork, my
grandmother Bejirond Yetemegnu, my brother Mesfin Zelleke

2. Family: from left to right my father, my mother, my grandmother Woizero
Tsedale Atchamyeleh, my sister Mekdes-Work, my uncle Lij Worku Gobena

3. Young Imru

4. Imperial Visitors, Vevey, Switzerland: L toR, Dejazmach Kassahun Hailu, HIH Prince Asfaw Wossen Haile Selassie in the light cape, Dejazmach Abera Kassa, myself, Ras Desta Damtew, my sister Ketsela, HIH Princess Tenagne Work, my father Bejirond Zelleke

5. 1928, Paris: L to R - My father as Envoy Extraordinary and
Minister Plenipotentiary to France and the United Kingdom, and
Ethiopia's Representative to the League of Nations; standing next to
him Ato Tesfaye Tegegn, First Secretary at the Paris Legation

CHAPTER 9

My First Years as a Diplomat

~

IN THE SPRING OF 1945, an Ethiopian delegation led by *Ras Bitwoded* Makonnen Endalkachew, then Prime Minister, went to San Francisco to represent Ethiopia at the first post-World War II Conference of Nations after the League of Nations had collapsed, and to sign the Charter that established the new world organization known as the United Nations. Once the Charter was signed, the conference decided to hold the first General Assembly of the Organization in London in September 1945. Our delegation to the General Assembly was led by Vice-Foreign Minister Aklilou Habte-Wold with *Tsehafi-Taezaz* Tefera-Work Kidane-Wold and comprised *Blatta* Ephrem Tewolde-Medhin, then Minister in London; *Bitwoded* Zewde Gabre-Hiwot, then First Secretary in London and myself as Secretary of the delegation. We carried a lot of documentation pertaining to our claims for war damages and the return of Eritrea. In fact, a Green Book had been prepared to detail the history of the Eritrean case in which were listed the names of several hundred Eritreans in high positions in the Ethiopian government. The claim for Eritrea's return to the motherland was motivated by these factors: a) undeniable historical facts; b) a strong Eritrean popular movement for unity with Ethiopia; c) the return of Ethiopia's legitimate access to the sea; d) all attempts at invasion have always taken place through that territory, so it was a primary strategic area; and e) a desire to vindicate the latent contention that the Shewan monarchy had sold Eritrea out to the Italians. As I mentioned earlier, a mission led by the Duke of Harar accompanied by two eminent Eritreans, Dr. Ambaye Wolde-Mariam, and Colonel Kassa Abraha, had been sent to Asmara to establish contacts with the Eritrean people as early as 1942.

Vice-Minister Aklilou Habte-Wold, *Tsehafi-Taezaz* Tefera-Work and I traveled from Addis Ababa to attend the conference in London, where we were joined by Ambassador *Blatta* Ephrem Tewolde-Medhin and *Bitwoded* Zewde Gabre-Hiwot. Our journey had been tiring and arduous; we had traveled by military transport planes whenever space was available. We flew from Addis Ababa to Cairo via Hargeisa, Aden, Khartoum, and Wadi Halfa. We stopped over in Wadi Halfa for a couple of days because our plane needed some maintenance. Wadi Halfa, a dusty little town on the Egyptian-Sudanese border was a railway station for the Anglo-Egyptian Railways and had also become a sort of hub for military air traffic. We stayed in a hotel run by the Railways. The menu in the restaurant was strictly British. With all the heat and the sand dust that was swirling around under the fans, we were served soup, Irish stew with boiled potatoes and puddings. With proper British stiff-upper-lip, everybody ate the sand-sprinkled warm food with dignity and style. Years later I stayed at the Railways' Grand Hotel in Khartoum, where the menu was still the same, less the sand.

Arriving in Cairo, we were held up for over a week awaiting available transport. We caught up with *Ato* Tesfaye Tegegn, Minister to Paris, and *Lij* Fasil Shiferaw, Second Secretary, *en route* to their posts. Due to the war, Cairo had become an important military center for the North Africa campaign and the Allied invasion of Europe from the South. It was also a very important transit point between East and West. The town was booming with all the income that thousands of soldiers and the military activity were generating. The war having ended, people were looking for peace and a bright future; all around the mood was joyous and exhilarating. All sorts of goods were available, so I bought some clothes which I badly needed. Eventually, some space was found for us on a military transport aircraft, and we flew to London *via* Marseille. The plane had no heating and was full of cargo; we were sitting on some makeshift seats amongst airplane parts. Fortunately, they had provided us with winter clothes and boots without which we would have frozen.

London was grim, cold and rainy. The damages of the war were visible everywhere. Everything was strictly rationed - food, drinks, clothes, fuel and so forth. We stayed at the Mayfair Hotel in the West End and were allocated offices close by, in a building on Grosvenor Square. The Assembly began soon after our arrival. After all the major speeches had been made, we adjourned to the Steering Committee where the agenda of the session was to be set up. Our principal concern was to put the Ethiopian case on the agenda of the Assembly and not have it postponed to a future meeting. In this our delegation was successful. Vice-Foreign Minister Aklilou had met and established good relations with all the world leaders in San Francisco, which I believe facilitated his task in presenting our case. My duties were to keep the office running and as usual ciphering and deciphering the many lengthy messages between Addis Ababa and us. At that time our code was a rather old system, and writing it was complicated and time-consuming. Otherwise, I cannot say that I had much to do with the workings of the various commissions. Other people who assisted with their advice were Mrs. Sylvia Pankhurst, Professor Jevons and Professor Faitlovitch, both old Fabians. Ms. Taylor, the Secretary at the Legation, a very kind and most helpful lady, never tired of our many personal requests.

London opened a new world for me, both intellectually and emotionally. Although it was not my first exposure to European culture, it was the first time as an adult. I was also fortunate that I was there under most favorable conditions as a diplomat with status and privileges, and even better, at a world conference where most of the great statesmen of the time were present. The British government had assigned people to facilitate our stay and show us around. The person that was assigned to us was a very nice elderly lady. Thanks to her, I was able to see the Shakespeare plays Richard II, Richard III, and Hamlet at the Old Vic Theater. Some of the court scenes in the plays reminded me of our own palace life; I could almost juxtapose some of the characters to those in our Court. I also attended a concert at the Royal Albert Hall. As I mentioned, food, drinks, clothing and many other goods were strictly rationed. Yet, although the worst had happened and it was a very difficult time, the war had been won and spirits were very high. The resilience and spiritual strength of the British people were really admirable. Another big event that had been organized besides the UN meeting was the Victory Parade in which contingents of all Allied military forces were to march. While our superiors had proper invitations, we - the staff - rented window space in private homes (fifty pounds per person) to watch the parade. Unfortunately, it rained cats and dogs on the day of the parade. What we saw were soldiers drenched in the rain miserably marching by and probably cursing their bad luck. An Ethiopian unit took part in the parade too, led by Major-General Tedla Makonnen, an eminent patriot leader.

~

The first General Assembly of the UN closed sometime in the third week of December 1945. The fate of former enemy colonial territories was left to the Four Great Powers, and it was to be discussed further at the Peace Conference to be held in Paris in April 1946. Vice-Foreign Minister Aklilou, *Tsehafi-Taezaz* Tefera-Work and I proceeded from London to Paris where preparations for the Peace Conference were being worked out. *Ato* Tesfaye Tegegn our Ambassador, *Ato* Seifu Yinessu and *Kegnazmach* Fasil Shiferaw were already there. They had opened the Embassy in the Hotel Lancaster in Rue de Berry. Although Paris had not suffered the kind of bombing that London did, housing was scarce, and many buildings had no heating. Food was rationed, and there were shortages of all sorts. However, unlike London, restaurants served two menus: one official and the other (better one) with black market prices. Otherwise, life was more or less coming together.

Then, Vice-Foreign Minister Aklilou had discussions with the French Minister Georges Bidault, and a few days later left for Ethiopia with *Tsehafi-Taezaz* Tefera-Work. I remained in Paris following up the preparations for the Peace Conference. During those few months in Paris, I had a lot of free time. I roamed around Paris and made many friends and acquaintances. I also went through new experiences that were deeply influential throughout my life. In the post-war period, the political atmosphere was very tense between the Right and the Left. General De Gaulle was in power, and the Communists and Socialists dominated a large bloc of the political spectrum. There were also the Vichyists - followers of Maréchal Pétain - who had collaborated with the Germans and were considered traitors. Several times, I saw people making citizens arrests of alleged collaborators and on a couple of occasions witnessed some women who had their hair shaved in public for having fraternized with the enemy. It is said that some forty thousand people were killed out of revenge during that period. The intellectual ambiance was very prolific. Existentialism was on the ascent, and in general, the Left Avant-Garde was at the forefront of the post-war cultural movement. The exposure to all these ideas and dialogues was an exhilarating experience that gave me a whole new vision of the world. I could even say that I acquired a new social conscience and a new perspective on our own society and political make-up. I was reading voraciously - newspapers, magazines, books and any writings I could lay my hands on.

The atmosphere at the Peace Conference was extremely lively. The negotiations of the Peace Treaty were complex, and the confrontation between East and West was fierce. Even the smallest item caused lengthy debates. As there was no simultaneous interpreting at the time, sessions took a very long time with the reading of statements from, or into, English, French, and Russian. Our delegation was composed of highly experienced diplomats. Besides *Tsehafi-Taezaz* Aklilou Habte-Wold, there were *Blatten-Geta* Lorenzo Taezaz, *Ato* Tesfaye Tegegn, *Blatten-Geta* Ephrem Tewolde-Medhin, and *Tsehafi-Taezaz* Tefera-Work Kidane-Wold. I list them by their later formal titles, but at the time they were all *Ato* except for Lorenzo Taezaz, who had the title of *Blatten-Geta*. Other members of the delegation were *Lij* Membere Yayehirad, *Sheikh* Haji Fara, and another Muslim member whose name escapes me. Lorenzo Taezaz was a French-educated lawyer who had served as Foreign Minister for the Emperor during exile and occupied the same post for a short spell after the Liberation. He had been one of the few of the Emperor's emissaries who had performed clandestine missions to organize the Resistance in Ethiopia during the Italian occupation. He had somehow fallen into disfavor with the Emperor, despite the fact that he was a real national hero, and had been sent away from Court as Ambassador to Moscow. It was from there that he joined us in Paris at the Conference. There was some unease with his presence. Aklilou, who had a high regard for him, was somewhat embarrassed at being his superior as head of the delegation. For his part, Lorenzo did not appear to be in good health. I believe he was also unhappy about the whole matter of his exile to Moscow and his exclusion from the central government, for which he had sacrificed so much. In any event, he did not stay long with us. He returned to Moscow where he died of some ailment after a short while. He was a very kind and erudite person whom I had known from my early youth. He always advised me to complete my education.

Future Prime Minister Aklilou was a very intelligent, gracious and kind person. A graduate of the Sorbonne in International Law as well as the *Ecole des hautes études commerciales de Paris;* he was well-versed in international affairs. He had served as Chargé d'affaires in Paris during the period of the Emperor's exile. I met him through my brother Mesfin Zelleke. They were both students in France and had become friends. Many French-educated professionals met at Aklilou's house. I used to go frequently to these reunions and was more or less adopted by the whole crowd. Aklilou was not good at reading written speeches; he was much better at speaking spontaneously. On a one-to-one basis, he was brilliant and could convince anyone of his argument. Thus he made an excellent impression on all the statesmen he met - even the formidable Soviet Minister Molotov - and established friendly relations with them. These personal qualities helped enormously in presenting our demands and obtaining support from many sides. Ephrem Tewolde-Medhin and Tesfaye Tegegn were old-hand diplomats who had served in London and Paris respectively. Tesfaye had accomplished many missions with Ethiopian delegations abroad before the Italian occupation. Tefera-Work was Private Secretary of the Emperor, so he was knowledgeable about the working habits of the Emperor. They did well in the various committees they attended, particularly *Blatta* Ephrem Tewolde-Medhin. After many negotiations amongst the Big Powers as to who would chair the Disarmament Committee, Ethiopia turned out to be acceptable for both sides and was elected as such. Thus Ephrem assumed the chairmanship of the Committee, which he handled most skillfully and with great tact, to the credit of our country. I attended some of the sessions, which for the person chairing were like walking in a minefield, with endless arguments and altercations between the two blocks, at times each side accusing the Chair of bias. It was a very tough assignment. My job was to run around the various committees and update the Minister as to what was going on in order to coordinate the work of our delegation. Also, I did all the coding of confidential messages. I leave the details of the Conference to other historians. I think that *Ato* Zewde Retta has done a magnificent work of it in his book in

Amharic, "*YeErtra Gudaye*" ("The matter of Eritrea"). The claims to Eritrea were many; at one point even Molotov said, "If charity begins at home, why not Eritrea for Russia?" Eventually, Italy was forced to renounce any claim on her former colonies, and the matter was passed to the Four Major Powers for their decision.

The Paris Peace Conference lasted from April to December 1946. The French Government should be complimented for the organization and set-up of the meeting. Despite the scarcities of the post-war period, everything was laid down to the highest standards and the entertainment offered to the delegates was magnificent. Free opera and theater tickets were offered, including the use of the presidential box at the Paris Opera. A splendid occasion was a reception held at the Palais du Luxembourg Gardens during which the Ballet de l'Opéra staged a magnificent show. Of course there were some minor hitches; for example, the opening of the conference was slightly delayed because not all the delegates had arrived in time for the opening. The reason was that the drivers of the cars assigned to each delegation were from military units, and unfamiliar with Paris streets. There were also some light moments during the conference. One day, all sorts of advertisements appeared around Paris with the word "GARAP," which nobody understood. Apparently, it was a publicity stunt made by a commercial enterprise. However, with their usual humor, French satirists coined it into "*Georges a recommencé à picoler*" ("George has started boozing"), making it a joke about the French Foreign Minister Georges Bidault, who was known to like his wine.

As for our delegation, everything was fine, and on the whole, our performance was good. The Emperor was obviously keeping close control of our doings, because the two Ambassadors Ephrem and Tesfaye, and Tefera-Work as his man at hand, were reporting to him directly on their own. Thus Aklilou was effectively walking a tight-rope, which obviously he managed adroitly. I believe that it was due mostly to his straightforward character. Whatever the case, he also had the protection of his older brother *Ato* Makonnen Habte-Wold, a great favorite of the Emperor, and his mentor *Tsehafi-Taezaz* Wolde-Giorgis, then Minister of the Pen and the most powerful man in the country. After the conference, while the others flew back by air, due to the voluminous documentation that we had to bring home and the scarcity of air facilities, *Lij* Membere and I had to go by rail to Marseille and board a boat to Alexandria. We took a rather small boat overcrowded with Egyptians returning home after being held up in Europe by the war. The journey was terrible. We had the misfortune of encountering a very violent storm in the Mediterranean which forced the boat to take refuge in Naples for about three days. At last, we managed to get home after some tribulations with the Egyptian customs which wouldn't release our baggage, despite our diplomatic status. Eventually, we settled the matter by paying the usual baksheesh.

For me, everything that had happened amounted to a tremendous and tumultuous experience. It was like a crash-course on many subjects simultaneously. It was not only the knowledge I acquired through witnessing both the UN General Assembly and the Peace Conference, but also the experience of post-war Europe where the political and social atmosphere was in full explosion. The ideological and political battle between the Right and Left was raging. In England, the Socialists had come to power. There was also the large presence of Americans who made a strong impact with their direct cultural and business styles, and particularly their plain and informal ways that were new to Europeans who were rather formal in their relationships. High-ranking American officials relating on a first-name basis with the lower ranks was very strange to them, for example.

⁓

As mentioned, my sojourn in Paris, of which I had a scant memory from my childhood, had the greatest impact on me. I had made several friends in the diplomatic and political circles. Whenever I could, I went to the famous Café de Flore in Saint-Germain-des-Prés where many well-known authors and artists such as Sartre, de Beauvoir, Camus, Prévert and many others kept court. Intense debates and arguments on all sorts of subjects from literature, music, painting, philosophy, society and politics went on. I was listening and absorbing all of it in a jumble without the scholastic discipline that could have allowed me to digest all this information in an orderly manner. Although I was carried away by all these trends, my traditional background kept me from going overboard and losing my identity. In a sense, my lack of formal education was a blessing in disguise, as it contained me within my roots, unlike many Ethiopian intellectuals educated abroad who found our traditional ways intolerable and not conforming to their newly acquired perceptions. Although they originate from common Judeo-Christian sources, the contrasts, and contradictions between our spiritual civilization and the more scientifically inclined ways of the Western world are sometimes so deep, that the choice seems to be to negate one or the other. Impressed by the great material and scientific achievements of the West, our educated class more often than not tended to ignore, if not disdain, our values in favor of foreign ones, probably because of a sense of superiority that foreign knowledge gave them. Therein, I think, is the misconception about civilization and modernity, which have different values and visions of their own. Our Ethiopian civilization is second to none regarding morals and manners. I think it was a French philosopher that said: "Civilization is not the discovery of the wheel or steam power, but the diminishing of original sin." It is not the lack of piety and prayers, nor the absence of civility that make-up our shortcomings, but rather the abandonment of our specific ethos (core values), for so-called modernity in which our role has been extremely minimal.

CHAPTER 10

Ethiopia in the International Community

~

WHEN I RETURNED HOME, I continued working as Secretary to the Minister and set about organizing a new International Organizations Department. In the meantime, preparations related to the Eritrean issue where being carried out intensely, and a Liaison Office headed by Colonel Nega Haile-Selassie (later Lt. General) was established in Asmara. In July 1947, *Bitwoded* Zewde Gabre-Hiwot was recalled from Stockholm where he was Chargé d'affaires, and I was appointed in his place. Ethio-Swedish relations were very close even before the Italian occupation; a Swedish military mission had helped establish the Holeta Military Academy, some Swedish medical doctors started the Haile Selassie Hospital, and several Swedish missionaries were working in the country. The Crown Prince of Sweden, later King Gustaf, had attended the coronation of the Emperor in 1930 and had established friendly ties with him. After the Liberation, because of its neutrality, Sweden was the first country from where Ethiopia sought assistance. A Swedish Military Mission had started training the Imperial Guard. Count Von Rosen, a world-famous aviator who had flown for the Red Cross during the Italian invasion, had returned to Ethiopia and was trying to re-organize the Air Force. His father, Count Von Rosen, was from the old Swedish nobility. Goering was married to his wife's sister, and it is said that he designed the Nazi cross. He was an extraordinary adventurer who had walked from Cape to Cairo in the early 1920s.

At that time the political relations of Sweden with the victorious Allies were rather cold. While Norway and Denmark were occupied by Hitler and fought against him along with the democratic alliance, Sweden remained neutral and had been trading with and supplying materials to Germany throughout the war. In general, Swedes sympathized with Germany and its culture. The second language spoken in Sweden was German, and the third French; very few people spoke English. However, none of this affected our relations with Sweden that had begun soon after our liberation.

Some twenty Saab training aircraft were purchased and were to be sent to Ethiopia. Several medical doctors and missionaries had also returned. Sweden was a novel experience for me. As I was involved in signing contracts for the Air Force and other technical personnel, I became interested in aviation and joined the Stockholm Royal Air Club where I took the training and received a private pilot's license. One day, Count Von Rosen came to our office and asked me to sign contracts for some people he had hired for the Air Force. According to the list he gave me, they were all majors and captains of the Swedish Air Force. However, when I checked their passports, I saw that they were all retired non-commissioned officers who were not fully qualified for the jobs for which they were being hired. He had simply promoted them on his own because they had worked for him at one time or another. This was not acceptable given my responsibilities, and I declined his request. I wrote to His Majesty and suggested that we request the Swedish Air Force to take up the training of our Air Force, rather than people being hired haphazardly. The Emperor agreed and gave me the go-ahead. While this was going on, *Blatta* Ephrem Tewolde-Medhin, our Ambassador in London who was also accredited to Sweden, came to Stockholm. It was fortunate that he did so, because after I had explained the matter to him he agreed, and we were able to raise the issue on his visit to Prime Minister Erlander after the presentation of his credentials to the

King. The Prime Minister consented to our request and authorized the Commander of the Swedish Air Force to proceed. Thus, a Colonel Berg was assigned to organize the Ethiopian Air Force. Officers from the Swedish Air Force took responsibility for the training of the personnel and the organization of the Air Force in a very professional manner. It was a very successful venture that gave Ethiopia a first class Air Force and provided professionally trained flying manpower to Ethiopian Airlines.

As the requirements for the Air Force developed further, a squadron of Saab B-17 fighter-bombers was purchased. They were flown to Ethiopia by Swedish Air Force personnel. On their return, the plane that was transporting them crashed on a mountain in Italy - a very tragic occurrence in which all the pilots and support personnel perished. For the first time in my life, I delivered a mass eulogy when the remains were repatriated to Sweden.

In the summer of 1948, I was ordered to go immediately to Prague where the appropriate instructions would be waiting for me. When I arrived in Prague, I met with a Mr. Cermakian, an Armenian businessman who had arranged the purchase of an ammunition factory and some armaments including light tanks. My job was to control the material and survey its shipment. This was a matter completely out of my competence. I immediately sent a telegram asking that a person with some expertise, possibly a military man, be sent to accomplish the task. I was replaced by a Swedish officer and traveled back to Stockholm. At that time the situation in Czechoslovakia was very tense. It was said that the Prime Minister, Mr. Masaryck, had committed suicide by jumping from his office window, which nobody I met believed to be true. The Communists had taken power despite the presence of the legitimate President of the country, Mr. Benecz. I had seen both of them in London and Paris during the UN Assemblies, where it was clear that they were under severe stress. Mr. Benecz had supported Ethiopia against the Italian invasion, and their delegation had continued to do so during the Paris Peace Conference.

As soon as I returned to Stockholm, I was recalled and instructed to join the Ethiopian delegation that was presenting the claims to Eritrea at the Four Powers meeting about the former Italian colonies in London. The meeting took place at Church House, the headquarters of the Church of England, where rooms had been made available. The weather was unusually hot. *Ato* Aklilou read an eighty-six-page long presentation of the Ethiopian claim. It was a great performance on his part, but highly exhausting for all present because of the heat, also because he was a slow reader. Eventually, the Four Powers decided to pass on the matter of disposal of former Italian colonies to the United Nations, and we traveled to Paris, where the General Assembly was due to be held in September 1948.

~

I was happy to return to the Paris that I loved. Paris is unique, and a beautiful, enchanting city. There is nothing like it on Earth. The ambiance is always electric; you hear more wit expressed walking a block in Paris than anywhere else in the world. Of course, you must know French to understand and catch the humor or innuendo of it. The French grumble about everything and are generally impatient. To get along, you have to behave the same way and be moderately strung out all the time, which is rather tiring. Otherwise, they are most charming, but not overly generous. When it comes to politics, the argumentation is to the death. Otherwise, they are refined and most civilized, and it is not for nothing that they are the world hub for elegance and fashion.

By 1948, life in Paris had normalized. There was no more rationing; almost everything was available. Politics were raging, and the arts, literature, theater, music and the cinema had acquired a febrile vitality born from the tragic experiences and deprivation of the war years. For me, life was as exciting and interesting as it could possibly be. I had made some good friends, including Jean Lessay, a professional journalist and correspondent for *l'Illustration* magazine. He had become the Press Attaché at our Embassy. He was a highly refined intellectual who was married to Cécile, one of three sisters of exceptional beauty, the daughters of French nobleman, Monsieur de Robillard who had married an Ethiopian lady. Their father had been in Ethiopia working for the Franco-Ethiopian Railways. Jean Lessay was really my mentor in understanding European politics and culture. He also introduced me to what one would call "the Cinema," a culture that was flourishing both in Europe and America. Unlike present times, the post-war cinema was a messenger of a new consciousness and reflective of a sweeping transformation brought about by a period of huge social disruption, physical destruction, and death. The '*cinéma vérité*' in France and the 'neo-realistic' school in Italy had come to be the new trend. In the same way, films produced in America mirrored the realities of the time. Jazz music in Paris was also flourishing. Many African-American musicians and artists, beginning with the famous Josephine Baker, had moved to Paris, which had a tradition of welcoming black artists. With the advent of the Socialist Party coming to power in Britain, the general political trend of the European intelligentsia was very much to the Left, so were my inclinations. Lessay, on the other hand, as a professional journalist knew the political ideologies, the parties, and the personalities at play intimately. He was not a leftist; he was rather of the Center and a patriot. His working at our embassy proved very valuable. Jean Ouannou had also joined the staff of our Embassy as Commercial Attaché. He was of Lebanese origin and had visited our country before the occupation when he helped establish the Franco-Ethiopian Chamber of Commerce. He also knew my father from his days as Minister of Commerce.

Another friend was Nico Papatakis, who was born from Greek and Ethiopian parents. The family owned the Majestique Hotel in Addis Ababa on Haile Selassie *Godana* (Avenue) approximately where the Artistic building is today. The hotel was burned down in the riots that occurred when the Italians occupied Addis Ababa. His mother worked underground to assist the Patriot's movements throughout the Italian occupation. Nico, who had migrated to Djibouti during the Italian occupation, went to France after a tragic incident that happened in an altercation with an Italian in a coffee house in Djibouti. In France, he managed to survive the German occupation and made friends with the intellectual and artistic milieux. A very handsome man, he had also played some minor roles in a few movies. However, what made him famous was the ownership of the Rose Rouge, a theater/club from which the careers of several renowned artists such as Juliette Greco, Les Frères Jacques, and many others were launched. For years, it was the venue where to encounter the night owls of "*le Tout-Paris*" (everyone in Paris, i.e. the fashionable and the affluent). My life was absolutely hectic and full of excitement. Between work and my desire to see and learn everything, I believe that I slept not more than four hours a day.

After a protracted debate on how to dispose of the former Italian colonies, the 1948 UN General Assembly decided to forward the matter to the next Assembly to be held in New York in April 1949. Nevertheless, members of our delegation conducted an intense campaign presenting our claims to all UN members in every committee they sat on. Aklilou personally conducted a very vigorous campaign with foreign ministers, heads of delegations and high ranking personalities present at the meeting, including the Italian Foreign Minister. He met several times with many of them and was able to bring to our side some of the Latin American countries who were mostly favorable to Italy. Besides the Arab countries and Pakistan, the most fervent antagonists to our claims were from South America - notably Argentina. Mexico had always been friendly to Ethiopia, since back in the days of the League of Nations, and had opposed the Italian occupation of our country. But generally speaking, the immediate post-war political atmosphere was not favorable to our demands. The major colonial powers of France, Britain, Netherlands, Belgium and South Africa were still hanging onto their colonies. Independent movements such as those in Indochina, North Africa, and Sub-Saharan Africa were violently opposed by the former colonial rulers. In our case, the British, whose African policy was still heavily influenced by the Colonial Office and by local British colonial administrations, were always creating problems in a rather subtle manner. Also, the French did not manifest much favor for the liberation of the former Italian colonies. Although they wanted us to support the Palestinian cause, all the Arabs countries, spearheaded by Egypt, were against our claims to Eritrea. This made our position on the issue rather difficult, as we also had serious concerns about the fate of the long-established Ethiopian churches and religious community in Jerusalem. We also recognized that the State of Israel was born with the support of all Western powers and that nobody could do anything about it.

At this point, I would like to mention Mrs. Sylvia Pankhurst and her Fabian friends who had championed the Ethiopian cause by opposing the Italian invasion. As of that time they had conducted a relentless struggle in support of our country. I had the pleasure to meet her when we were in London. One day she invited us for tea, where we met her husband Mr. Corio and their son Richard, who was then a student. Mr. Corio was an Italian radical exiled in England because of his controversial politics in Italy. She was a very kind and valiant lady completely committed to the good of all people. She published a newspaper, the *New Times and Ethiopia News* in which she incessantly challenged and exposed the many errors of British policy all the way until the federation of Eritrea was achieved. Her mother - who was the famous suffragette Emmeline Pankhurst - and herself were well known in England for their activism. There is no doubt that she influenced British public opinion about Ethiopia.

As mentioned, the 1948 United Nations Special General Assembly was held in Paris and concluded without any decision about the ex-Italian colonies. It was during this session that a UN radio program was initiated in the Amharic language. *Ato* Seyfu Yinessu was the speaker. I returned to Addis Ababa with the rest of the delegation. Meanwhile, the Unionist Party in Eritrea had been very active. *Ato* Amde-Mikael Dessalegn had taken over the Liaison office in Asmara. I went to Asmara with Prime Minister Aklilou, where various aspects of the political situation were discussed with the heads of the Unionist Party, other Eritrean personalities, the head of the British Military Administration General Cumming, and the Italian representative in Asmara. We established close coordination between our Liaison Office in Asmara and our Foreign Office. Members of a delegation of the Unionist Party were selected that would attend the 1949 UN General Assembly under the leadership of *Dejazmach* Tedla Bairu, President of the Party.

CHAPTER 11

Mission to Latin America

~⌒

IN VIEW OF THE STRONG relationship that Italy had with the Latin American countries, it was decided that an Ethiopian mission should be sent to South America to establish an understanding with some of these nations about our claim that Eritrea should be reunited with the motherland. The idea of sending a mission was also suggested to Aklilou by some friendly Latin American foreign ministers, who felt that a personal contact with some of the Heads of State might subdue the Latin American group's opposition to our cause. Brazil, Chile, Peru, Venezuela, and Mexico responded favorably to our visit. Argentina declined our request but allowed us to transit through on our way to Chile. The preparations for an official visit were rather complicated. Once a favorable answer was received, a personal letter from the Emperor to the country's Head of State had to be written, and position papers and documentation concerning Ethiopia's cause had to be prepared by us. Decorations and medals to be bestowed to high officials during the visit had to be collected according to the rank of the officials to be decorated in each country. As officials love decorations to hang on their chest, the lists of recipients were quite long - averaging around ten people per country. This entailed a lot of labor in preparing certificates for each decoration that had to be written by hand in classic Amharic calligraphy (*yequm tsihfet*) on special parchment paper to be signed by the Emperor.

The Ministry of Pen was the holder of all Orders and Honorific titles. Feleke Irgetu, who was then Secretary-General of the Ministry of Pen, had everything prepared in a most efficient manner.

The mission was headed by Foreign Minister Aklilou Habte-Wold and Ambassador Tesfaye Tegegn, our Ambassador in France, as his second, and myself as Secretary. There was nothing glamorous about my functions; I did all the secretarial work, typing, coding messages, checking flights and hotel reservations, and taking care of the baggage which by that time amounted to a dozen large cases of official paraphernalia plus five of our own. If you think that gallivanting around South America with eighteen pieces of luggage in antiquated airplanes - mostly DC3's - is amusing, you should try it; departing from London *via* Lisbon and Dakar to Rio de Janeiro, the journey took about thirty-six hours.

In Rio, we were received with great warmth. Visits to the President, the Parliament, and high officials went very smoothly, together with receptions, dinners, luncheons and sundry functions. Actually, an Italian mission had preceded us in campaigning around South America. They had convinced the governments that there were some three hundred thousand Italian colonists in the ex-colonies and that there was a human factor involved in removing them. They maintained that they were the main economic sustainers of the territories, and their transfer to Ethiopia would cause a social and economic disaster. These absurd lies caused serious consternation with the officials we met. They changed their mind and promised their support when Minister Aklilou explained that during the sixty years of colonial rule, prior to the invasion of Ethiopia in 1935, there were no more than a couple of thousands of Italians in Eritrea and maybe one thousand in Somalia. The three hundred thousand Italians were military and civilians brought in for the occupation, and these had been evacuated by the British as soon as Ethiopia was liberated. He explained that at present, there were no more than fifteen thousand Italians in Ethiopia and Eritrea mostly engaged in business.

One thing that puzzled us was that the Brazilian officials we met were mentioning an Ethiopian goodwill mission that had preceded ours. When we told them that no such delegation had been sent from Ethiopia, they remained as perplexed as we were. We stayed four days in Rio and on the last day, the desk called me saying that a certain Mr. Shalaby wanted to see the Minister. We were surprised since we didn't know anyone in Rio, so I went downstairs to meet him. He was a short, dapper man of Egyptian origin. He told me that he was a journalist and that he was appointed by our Ministry of Information as a correspondent for the Ethiopian newspapers. He showed me an official letter from the Ministry of Information signed by *Ato* Amde Mikael Dessalegn, then Director-General of the Ministry, appointing him and Fawzi Hanna Salim as Ethiopian press correspondents. Shalaby said that he had been promised by our Ministry of Information that payments will be made for articles he wrote about Ethiopia and that he had not been paid. He showed me copies of several articles he had published in the Brazilian papers. The articles were really good; I took them to show to the Minister, who liked them as I did, and asked to see the man. Shalaby, a smooth talker, explained to the Minister that he was in some difficulty because the promised payments were delayed and that he needed help. Minister Aklilou was quite impressed and promised that he would take some action when he returned home. In the meantime, he ordered to me to give him four hundred US dollars, which was quite a sum in those days.

Rio is a beautiful town. We stayed in the old part, at the Hotel Gloria, a high-class establishment in the old European style. Copacabana was the newest modern part of the city. We visited some museums. A most spectacular view of Rio and its bay was from where the famous statue of Christ is situated above the city on Corcovado Mountain. Otherwise,

I did not see much of the city; I was headquartered in my hotel room coding messages and arranging our next journey, except for one occasion when a young man who was our escort took us to where there were many shops selling precious stones, which were abundant in Brazil. Our visit was very successful. After many meetings with officials and politicians, the Brazilian government agreed to support our cause, despite a lot of pressure from Italy and some of the Latin American countries supporting them.

On the fourth day in Rio, we departed for Chile, via Buenos Aires. Argentina, of which half of the population was probably Italian, declined to meet our delegation but allowed us to transit through. In Buenos Aires, because of our voluminous baggage, we had to wait two days to get a connection to Santiago. We stayed in a beautiful English style hotel; I think it was called the Alvear. Eventually, we managed to get seats on an old DC3 that commuted between the two cities. In the meantime, our stay in Buenos Aires was quite eventful. The next day after our arrival, the front desk called me and said that we had some visitors waiting in the lobby. I was quite surprised because our trip had not been announced. When I got downstairs, the concierge took me to a sitting room off the lobby where some twenty-five men and women were waiting. I introduced myself as Secretary to the Minister, and in turn, some of them introduced themselves as Honorary Consuls-General of Ethiopia, one for Cultural Affairs, the other for Commerce, for Mining, for Agriculture, etc. I was dumbfounded. I said that I was not aware of their appointments, and asked how they had received such titles. They told me that it was the Special Representative of the Emperor who had bestowed them the titles and produced letters attesting to that claim. What had happened was that Shalaby and Fawzi Hanna Salim had taken the letter given to them by *Ato* Amde Mikael, retained the Lion on the letterhead, erased the part that said "Ministry of Information", and substituted it with "Imperial Ethiopian

Government - Special Representative of H.I.M. Haile-Selassie to Latin America". They had also written Amharic text of their own, appointing Shalaby as Head of a Goodwill Ethiopian mission to Latin America. Thus armed, they had gone to Brazil where they were received with great honors. Shalaby had even spoken to the Parliament, had given interviews to the media, and had borrowed money from some people telling them that funds would arrive soon. In Argentina, he did the same and received money for each appointment he was making. Then he organized a whole group of artists, painters, sculptors, musicians and told them that the Emperor had invited them to stage a cultural exhibition in Addis Ababa. He also told them that a ship had been chartered to take them and their material to Ethiopia. The poor fellows had gone to a lot of expense and effort to pack their works. Then Shalaby told them that the chartered ship was delayed because the payment had not arrived due to the difficulty of transferring money from Africa, and asked them if they could advance the money which would be returned as soon as they arrive in Ethiopia. This done, Fawzi disappeared to Uruguay and Shalaby went into hiding in Brazil, where he had married a Brazilian woman to avoid extradition. Unfortunately, there was nothing we could do for those unfortunate people who had been duped with the title of "Honorary Consul."

～

Our flight to Santiago was highly dramatic. The DC3 in which we were traveling could not fly high enough over the Andes, so the aircraft was following some gorges. The mountain peaks were above us, and sometimes we were so close to the sides it looked as if the wings would touch them. We were buffeted up and down by the winds until we crossed the Andean mountain range and eventually landed in Santiago. It was one of the scariest flights I have ever experienced.

In Santiago, another surprise was awaiting us. The Chief of Protocol who received us at the airport instead of the Minister of Foreign Affairs as is customary told us that there was a *coup d'état* going on and that there was no government at the moment. When we asked what we should do, he said that we should wait, because there is a chance that the ousted government might return. It was quite a shock, because the Chilean Foreign Minister had become good friends with our Minister during the many UN sessions, and he was a warm supporter of our cause. Moreover, all the diplomas for the medals we were to give were inscribed with the names of the officials to be decorated, which meant that we could not use them for anybody else, as it was impossible to erase the names written in *Ge'ez* letters. The Chief took us to our hotel and told us not to move, as the situation may change at any moment. Every so often they called from the Foreign Ministry and told us to hold on, and that matters would be settled soon. We were very worried because we still had to pay a visit to Peru, Venezuela, and Mexico before joining the UN General Assembly in New York. Time was getting short. On the fourth day, the Chief of Protocol came and told us that the old government had returned and that we should go immediately to the Palace to meet the President and others officials at a ceremony in which we could present the purpose of our mission and award the decorations. In the meantime, while we were waiting in Chile, a *coup d'état* had occurred in Peru, our next destination. The Minister decided that we should go there anyway because we needed their vote.

~

When we reached Lima, General Odria had taken power. Everything went with military efficiency. The next day we finished our business, with the General promising to support our claims. Nonetheless, the Peruvian Foreign Minister, Professor Belaunde, whom we had met while he was attending the various meetings at the UN, was not favorably inclined towards us and tended to side with Argentina and the Latin group supporting Italy. As usual, we attended the customary dinners, luncheons, and receptions. A very interesting place we visited was the University of St. Mark, which was the oldest University in the Americas. Another very impressive sight was a small town we visited up in the mountains. While the Argentine and Chileans were manifestly European, in Peru the indigenous Inca culture was visible in many of the artifacts and the architecture we saw. The traditional had blended beautifully with the Spanish import.

At this point some difficulties arose over our journey; we could not get a direct flight to Venezuela. We had to go first to Panama and try to find a flight from there. When we reached Panama, we were told that there were no flights available neither to Venezuela and nor to Mexico for at least one week. As a result, we had to abandon our visit to Venezuela and try to get at least to Mexico to be on time in New York. Thus, we were stuck in Panama for a week. We later found out that we were deliberately delayed because there was an Italian delegation visiting the two countries, and the two governments did not want us to be there at the same time. Panama then was a small town with no particular character to talk about. The only two remarkable features were the Canal and the American enclave. The climate was hot, and it rained continuously while we were there.

~

At last, after a boring six days in Panama, we were able to fly to Mexico City, where we received a very warm welcome. Since the days of the League of Nations, Mexico had defended Ethiopia against the Italian occupation and was a staunch supporter of our cause at the United Nations. Our visit was well organized, and we paid calls to the most important officials from the President down. All sorts of official functions, including tours of historical sites were organized for us. What impressed me the most were the Teotihuacan Aztec pyramids. I climbed one of them all the way to the top, but coming down was rather difficult because the steps were very high and steep, which I had not realized when going up. We also visited Cuernavaca, a beautiful resort town in the hills out of Mexico City. At the same altitude of Addis Ababa, the climate and vegetation of the Mexican high plateau resembled that of Ethiopia's landscapes. Amongst the various museums we visited, I was fascinated by the works of the modern painters, like José Clemente Orozco and Diego Rivera. We saw a huge mural by Diego Rivera on one of the walls of a new hotel; I think it was the Hilton. They had emptied the room of people before we saw the mural that was covered with curtains. The painting was depicting the Mexican Revolution. The problem was that in one part, Rivera had painted the figure of a child holding a banner that said: *"Dio non existe"* (God does not exist), which was anathema for the Catholic Church in Mexico. So it was sheltered from public view. He also painted a mural at the Rockefeller Center in New York, which Rockefeller ordered destroyed when he realized that Diego Rivera was a Communist.

As is well known, the Mexican Revolution (1910-1920) was very violent, particularly against the Church, where clergy were brutally persecuted. Of course, by the time we got there those conditions had passed many years before. Nevertheless, religious and revolutionary fervor were both very much alive amongst all classes. When I was in Sweden the first time, one of my good friends was Señor Ricardo Almanza, a Mexican diplomat. He was a radical Marxist and a highly cultured person. His girlfriend was a Hungarian baroness with all the aristocratic pedigree and bearing thereof. He also drove a Jaguar, which was a rarity in those days. We used to tease him because of the odd combination of his bourgeois tastes and his revolutionary rhetoric. The Mexican

Foreign Ministry, which did not lack a sense of humor, had transferred him to Moscow - imagine - Moscow in 1947! When I met him during our courtesy visit, I asked him how he had fared in Moscow. In reply, he mumbled something about which it seemed the Baroness and the Jaguar did not do so well. It also turned out that his Mexican revolutionary style did not fit in with the grim and humorless atmosphere of the Socialist "Paradise." To escape from this terrible predicament, he had expressed some pro-capitalist rhetoric, which caused his immediate transfer to Stockholm with the Baroness and the Jaguar.

In Mexico, a prominent and revered personality to whom we made a courtesy call was Judge Isidoro Fabela, who had retired from the International Court of Justice. Minister Aklilou knew him from the days of the League of Nations when he represented Mexico. His house, a beautiful example of Spanish colonial architecture, was full of precious Aztec artifacts. Although he had retired from public life, his support was very influential in the Mexican foreign policy milieu. Thus, having concluded our Latin America tour, we proceeded to New York for the UN session. In the end, our goodwill tour was very successful because we gained the support of all the countries we visited including Venezuela, even though we had had to cancel our visit there. Moreover, the countries we visited were the most prominent in the Latin American bloc and were very influential in the group, which enabled us to secure some more Latin votes.

CHAPTER 12

The United Nations

$\sim$

WE ARRIVED IN NEW YORK just in time for the opening of the 1949 UN General Assembly. The other members of our delegation were already there. However, we did not have enough people to cover all the various committees, even the six principal ones. For me, the workload had become overwhelming. In those days the UN met in Lake Success, on Long Island, in a facility that was built for a World Fair. We were lodged in New York City, which meant going back and forth to our office in town several times a day. We had Major Mesfin Begashet, who was First Secretary in our Embassy in Washington join us in New York and take over the secretariat of the delegation. My function was to coordinate the work in the various committees and report to the Minister whenever his decisions were required. I was also assigned to attend the Third Committee on Human Rights. This gave me a chance to attend some of the committee meetings and learn more about their procedures and the various subjects in their agenda. In addition to all this, I also started broadcasting for the UN Radio in Amharic from the ABC studios in Times Square, New York. The program aired at 1:00 a.m., a rather inconvenient time.

A most interesting debate took place in the Third Committee where the draft of the UN Universal Declaration of Human Rights was discussed. The strongest opposition to the Declaration came from the Soviet bloc, while most countries were in favor of adopting such an instrument.

The philosophical, ideological, moral and legal character of the debate over human rights was simply extraordinary. For a neophyte like me, it amounted to a university course in the humanities. Amongst the most vigorous advocates of the Declaration were Mrs. Eleanor Roosevelt, Ms. Indira Ghandi from India, and Dr. Charles Malik, Foreign Minister of Lebanon. As I was instructed to vote for the Western position generally, I had the opportunity to meet many of these people almost on a daily basis. Another of my duties was to arrange appointments with other delegates for our Minister. In those days the UN was not the caravanserai that it is nowadays, there were only fifty-two member nations, so it was easy to contact any of the delegates at any time.

The UN Session concluded by setting up a UN Commission for Eritrea to investigate the situation locally, and to report its findings to the next UN General Assembly. We rushed back to Addis to prepare for the visit of the Commission. This time I was charged to liaise with the Ministry of Information for Eritrean affairs, and also to be Chief of Protocol of the Ministry of Foreign Affairs. Protocol consisted of two departments. That of the Imperial Court came under the Ministry of the Palace and was in charge of all matters of domestic protocol, audiences, receptions, ceremonials, diplomatic functions, ranks and precedence and so forth. This was a very complex task, because of the many traditional practices and paradigms involved. However, matters regarding foreign relations were handled by the Private Secretary of the Emperor, who was then *Tsehafi-Taezaz* Tefera-Work Kidane-Wold, and the Protocol Department of the Ministry of Foreign Affairs was in charge of all matters concerning the Foreign Diplomatic Corps in Addis Ababa. At that particular time, there were very intense diplomatic as well as domestic activities because the UN Fact-Finding Mission for Eritrea was underway.

Almost the whole government was mobilized on the Eritrean issue. *Tsehafi-Taezaz* Wolde-Giorgis Wolde-Yohannes as Minister of the Pen and *Ato* Makonnen Habte-Wold as Minister of Information had done a magnificent job in mobilizing all national resources and public opinion to support the return of Eritrea to the motherland. I remember an instance when a Pakistani member of the UN Commission requested to interview the Muslim community in Ethiopia in order to hear their views on the Eritrea question. *Ato* Makonnen Habte-Wold organized a big meeting where some two hundred representatives from various Muslim communities were present. After interviewing several people, came the turn for Haji Bedasso, a senior leader of the community. The Haji told the Pakistani delegate that his family had been Muslims for generations, and how in Ethiopia Christians and Muslims had lived in peace and harmony for centuries, quoting the Koran and the Prophet's words about Ethiopia. He stated that he had lived freely doing whatever he liked, that he was respected and enjoyed the trust and courtesy of all. Then he concluded by saying that he had enjoyed several marriages, without anyone objecting or complaining about it. At this point, the interpreter, who was Ambassador Meles Andom (elder brother of General Aman Andom) felt embarrassed. As I was standing nearby, he asked me if he should interpret the last statement, I said, "Why not? It is the truth!". The statement upset the Pakistani delegate, who interrupted the interviews abruptly.

As I have said earlier, there was a lot of diplomatic activity against our cause at the time, especially by the Italians with whom we had not yet established diplomatic relations. There were still problems to be settled with them, mainly the question of war reparations and secondly the border with Somalia, which had come under their trusteeship. The Italians were dragging their feet on both matters. In Addis Ababa, they conducted a very strong lobbying effort directly with the Palace, by sending former diplomats to Ethiopia such as Cora, Piacentini, representatives of the Catholic Church that included several prominent Ethiopians, and some old foreign residents of Ethiopia like Dr. Zervos, a Greek medical doctor who was close to the Emperor.

Regarding the border with Somalia, I had suggested that we should not normalize our relations with the Somali since the Italians were the original signatories of the Treaty which they later negated. I advised that the matter should be settled with Italy, and not with the new government of independent Somalia and that if the border were to remain as is, it was likely to cause future frictions between the two countries. An inter-ministerial committee chaired by *Ato* Getahun Tessema was set up to study the issue and make recommendations. In fact, the committee suggested some very strong conditions, including the settlement of war reparations before the normalization of relations. But to the dismay of many of us, the 'Palace' lobby won the day. The Italian sent a goodwill mission led by a secondary official of their Foreign Ministry, and relations were established despite our strong opposition.

～

Returning to the Eritrea issue, the UN commission had returned to Eritrea and started its investigations. H.E. *Ato* Zewde Gabre-Hiwot (later *Bitwoded*) was then Vice-Minister at the Ministry of Foreign Affairs. He frequently went to Asmara to coordinate matters there with what was planned and done from Addis Ababa. Because the other Director-Generals in the Ministry were on mission or busy with other issues, I was often the sole senior official in the Ministry. On one occasion, after we had voted for the UN resolution to intervene militarily in Korea, the American Chargé d'Affaires came to see me and informed me verbally that the US would like Ethiopia to contribute to the war with a military contingent. When I reported this to the Emperor, he ordered me to communicate the request to Foreign Minister Aklilou, who was in New York at the time. Aklilou answered that we should give political and moral support to the UN decision, but that we should not intervene in the campaign with our troops. When I informed the Emperor of the Minister's answer, he asked me my personal view; I answered that the UN Commission for Eritrea had given a divided report that had rendered a decision in our favor in serious doubt. It was also clear that

a) without a strong backing from the US we could not win our cause; b) we also had a moral obligation to the Western powers because they fought for our liberation from Italy, and that we owe them our freedom; while we complained bitterly about our betrayal by the League of Nations, now it was our turn to stand up for the same principle of 'collective security' that we had claimed then; and c) our defense forces were likely to benefit from the experience, and also that it would provide us a way to improve the quality and quantity of our military equipment, and that therefore we should participate in the military action. The Emperor told me to wait for his decision.

I remember it was late afternoon, when the Emperor usually went out on his regular drive, visiting hospitals and performing other public functions. I was received in the small salon called the 'Blue Room' in the Palace, where years later Girmame Neway and company would murder many high officials. I waited for about two hours before being called in, and the Emperor told me to inform the Americans of his decision that Ethiopia will contribute a military battalion to the UN forces in Korea, and to convey the same to our Minister in New York. I guess that the Emperor had consulted some of the high officials, like *Ras* Kassa, *Ras* Abebe, and the military before making his decision. Following the Emperor's consent, a formal request was presented officially, which was nominally discussed and approved by the Crown Council and the Council of Ministers. I believe that it earned us the full support of the US with regard to the Eritrean question.

~

Another big event that I remember during that period was the separation of the Ethiopian Orthodox Church from the Egyptian Coptic Orthodox Church, which gave Ethiopia the right to nominate its own Patriarch, who formerly was appointed by the Egyptian Church. This matter had taken lengthy negotiations with the Egyptians who were adamant about relinquishing the grasp they had on the Ethiopian Church. Eventually, our *Liqe-Papasat, Abuna* Basilios, went to Alexandria, signed the Concordat between the two Churches, and was crowned Patriarch of Ethiopia. This was a great moment for the Ethiopian Church, which had suffered the dictates of the Alexandrian clergy for centuries. Gaining the independence of the Ethiopian Orthodox Church during his reign was another great historic achievement for Emperor Haile Selassie. A big ceremony was organized for the return of the new Patriarch. In the great hall of Menelik Palace all dignitaries, the Diplomatic Corps and foreign guests in uniform and regalia were assembled. Unfortunately, the plane was late, and everybody - including H.I.M. - had to stand and wait for almost an hour. Eventually, the Patriarch arrived. A twenty-one gun salute was to be fired before he made his speech. Then something funny happened. The Patriarch was standing in front of the Emperor with his written speech in his hand waiting for the cannons to fire, when instead of loud cannon shot, all that they heard was something like a big "puff" a couple of times. Obviously, the cannons were firing the wrong charge. H.I.M was furious, and so was the Minister of Defense and the Chief of Staff, and everybody down the line. It was like a movie scene to see every one of them scattering to find out what went wrong. It turned out later that the Ministry of Finance had cut off the budget for this item, and that the army had nothing but expired cannon charge for this type of event.

At this point, my personal life was also changing. I got engaged to *Woizerit* Martha Nassibou, daughter of *Dejazmach* Nassibou Zamanuel, whom I have mentioned earlier. I got married in the spring of 1950. I continued with the same job until the middle of that year, after which I was assigned to join our UN delegation in New York. This time I traveled with my wife (at our own expense of course). While I was working at the conference, Martha, a very gifted painter, who previously had attended art school in England, joined the New York Art Students League and continued her artwork. Having been in New York several times I knew my way around town, we therefore had a lot of social activity. We lived in a middle-size hotel-apartment near Gramercy Park. Between diplomatic functions at the UN and the zillion things that New York offers, we had a busy and most enjoyable time.

On one occasion Mrs. Eleanor Roosevelt invited all the members of the Third Committee for lunch at their country home in Hyde Park a couple of hours drive out of New York. It was a magnificent place. However, the luncheon, to the great disappointment of the guests, consisted of sandwiches and soft drinks, rather than the profusion of food and drink expected at a great house. Another time Mrs. Roosevelt invited some of the delegates including my wife and me to a private dinner at the house of one of her friends, a huge apartment on Park Avenue. I think that the lady of the house was a Morgan (of J.P. Morgan fame). She had a great collection of paintings, which must have been worth millions. She took us around the apartment and showed us the many paintings and artifacts of her collected works. That was very impressive. We toured the apartment until we reached her husband's office. In contrast to the rest of the house, the room was empty of any artwork, just white walls. He told us that he was a child psychiatrist and could concentrate better in that kind of environment. One of the guests told me that his study of child psychology was based on observing the behavior of chickens. A joke or not, I never knew. A most pleasant evening ended after Josh White, a famous Black guitarist, who was one of the guests, performed some songs of his repertoire. Amongst the many people we encountered in New York whom I distinctly remember was a person we met at a charity function, the Black actor Canada Lee, a former boxer who made history on stage playing white roles, with some sort of make-up, although he was even darker than I am. He was a very gentle person who introduced us to many of his artist friends. He had acted in Shakespeare plays and in a film titled "Life Boat" with Tallulah Bankhead. His story was rather tragic. It happened during the McCarthy era when anti-communism was raging in the United States. Because he refused to testify against Paul Robeson, Walter Winchell, a popular radio talk show person, accused him of being a leftist sympathizer, so he was blacklisted and could not get a job anywhere. He was banned from everywhere in the theater and film world. I think he died broken-hearted.

The United Nations finished its 1950 session by deciding that Eritrea join Ethiopia in a Federation. A special Committee was appointed to implement the resolution and finalize the union by the end of 1952. I cannot describe the elation and joy we felt at that moment. It was a victory for which so many people had worked so hard, and a great historical moment for us and the country. In the evening, we gathered in the Minister's suite at the Waldorf Astoria and toasted the event. All of us expressed our joy with various statements. The most touching was the one made by *Blatten-Geta* Ephrem Tewolde-Medhin, who recalled his escape to Ethiopia from Italian colonial rule years before, and said that he had always dreamt of a reunion of Eritrea with the motherland, and now, at last, the dream was going to come true. By that time my wife was seven months pregnant. I asked her if she would prefer to give birth to our child in New York, where there were better medical facilities than in Ethiopia, also because the return voyage was rather arduous. However, in spite of the risks and difficulties involved, she said that she didn't want her child to be born outside Ethiopia, and we returned home with some anxiety. Thus my first daughter, Adey Abeba, was born in Addis Ababa.

CHAPTER 13

Federation with Eritrea

~

THERE WAS GREAT JUBILATION IN Addis Ababa over the UN decision that Eritrea should join Ethiopia in a federation. The stature and prestige of Minister Aklilou Habte-Wolde were also much enhanced. The UN decision stipulated that all home affairs were the responsibility of the Eritrean government and that the Federal government would be responsible for foreign affairs, currency and finance, internal and foreign trade, customs, external and interstate communications, including ports, railways, aviation and defense. In preparation thereof, a new set of activities, in which many government ministries and departments were involved, was initiated immediately. These included the Federal Constitution to be negotiated with the UN Commission, the federal administrative structure, the handover from the British Military Administration, defense and security matters, laws and regulations, finance and banking, and many other aspects related to the integration of the two territories. Several inter-ministerial committees were formed to this end. I was acting as liaison with them and the Foreign Ministry, the Liaison Office in Asmara and the British authorities. I was going back and forth to Asmara and reporting to the Minister. Meanwhile, *Dejazmach* Kifle Yirgetu was appointed to head the handover Mission from the British and I became his deputy. Because of his many duties in Addis Ababa, *Dejazmach* Kifle was not as free to move as I was, and was kind enough to leave most of the detailed work to me. Department heads from each Ministry were selected and appointed to take charge of the federal administration.

While all this was being done, I had negotiated and taken over from the British Military Administration the physical facilities such as the Palace, and whatever remained in terms of offices, military installations, residential houses and other structures assigned to the federal administration. The British, under the guise of the Lend-Lease agreement entered into with the United States during WWII, had dismantled and destroyed many facilities built during the war such as Gura Airport, Massawa Naval Base and other major structures, including the floating dry dock anchored in Massawa which they sold to Pakistan. Nothing was left standing in the naval base but for a small Italian-built residence belonging to the base commander and an underground fuel storage used for submarines which the British officer in place wanted to dynamite though it was an Italian-built structure and not granted by the Lend-Lease Act. Although some British officials including their head, Major-General Cummings, appeared friendly and civilized, it is hard to explain their very strong antagonism towards Ethiopia. They destroyed, disabled and sold everything they could, including the remaining bricks and debris which they sold to local merchants. The only place in Eritrea that they maintained well was the British cemetery on the hills overlooking Keren, where for once the Italians had shown some stiff resistance in battle. Otherwise, it was the most systematic and methodical process of destruction ever undertaken to denude a territory of any structural viability. Knowing full well that we had limited resources, they created all sorts of stumbling blocks and difficulties for our takeover. Actually, after all that ruination, some British officials even had the gall to offer their services. We only employed one that could be helpful to us, Brigadier-General Stafford, who became an advisor to the Ministry of Finance in Addis Ababa.

The UN Commission that was to supervise the implementation of the federation arrived a couple of months after the UN decision, led by M. E. Matienzo, former Minister of Foreign Affairs of Bolivia, and opened their offices in Asmara. Discussions had started with the various political parties concerning the government of Eritrea. With regard to the Federal Constitution, discussions took place mostly in Addis Ababa. By that time, I had moved with my family and taken residence in Asmara because working out the many details of the handover involved a lot of traveling to the various installations in Dekemare, Massawa, Assab, Keren, Agordat, Tesseney and other places. Concerning defense, an advanced battalion from the Third Division of the Ethiopian Army under the command of Brigadier-General Kebede Abebe, was assigned to take over the various military installations in Eritrea. The Deputy Commander of the unit was Lieutenant-Colonel Abebe Gemeda (later Lt.-Gen. Commander of the Imperial Guard, murdered by the Derg) an officer we all admired for the efficiency and professionalism of his command.

~

The negotiations between ourselves, the UN Commission and the Eritrean political parties to establish the Federal Constitution and Administration were lengthy and difficult. On our part, we wanted the structures to be as close as possible in view of an eventual future integration, while the UN mission wanted to make the federal set-up as loose as possible, as some of the Eritrean anti-unionist parties wanted. Besides the negative interference by the British, instigated by the Italians and other countries, splits had started to appear amongst the various Eritrean political groups. As an Eritrean autonomous administration was to be established, the matter of power-sharing took center stage within the Eritrean political factions and personalities. The traditional clan contentions between Hamassien, Akele Guzay, and Serae in addition to those between Orthodox Christians, Catholics, Muslims, and Protestants came into play. Some were objecting strongly to the leadership of Tedla Bairu, President of the Unionist Party because he was a Protestant, while we supported him strongly because of his intellect and demonstrated leadership. Finally, we arrived at a formula that was agreeable to all parties and confirmed by the United Nations. Here, I must pay my highest compliments to the high diplomatic and political skills of the late *Ato* Amde-Mikael Dessalegn, head our Liaison Office in Asmara, who managed the compromises between the various groups skillfully and with grace, and established common grounds that allowed the formation of the Eritrean government. His wife, *Woizero* Zewditu Ambachew, must also be congratulated for her work in organizing endless receptions and for establishing close and friendly relations with the Eritrean women associations.

Meanwhile, there was a quite a lot of in-fighting going on between the various groups regarding who should be appointed as the Federal Representative in Eritrea. Unlike the usual appointment of a provincial Governor-General, this was a special position with a dual role of representing the Crown in the Federal Territory, as well as being in charge of the functions of the Federal Administration as prescribed by the Federal Constitution. This meant that the position had to be filled by a very senior member of the central government. As I was frequently going back and forth from Asmara to Addis Ababa, on one occasion the Emperor called me and said that he intended to appoint *Ras* Andargachew Messai to the post, and asked my views about it. I knew the *Ras* from childhood, and he was a good friend of my family, but I had never worked with him. I knew him as a well-intentioned, good person, so I had nothing to say, and answered that HIM knew him better than I did and that I had no suggestions to make. Obviously, the decision was already made, - because he then said "Anyway, we have already promised the position to Princess Tenagne Work," his eldest daughter and wife of *Ras* Andargachew. Personally, I was somehow apprehensive, because the *Ras* was not familiar with the many legal and administrative implications of the federal structure. Neither was he acquainted with the many Eritrean personalities and political groups that were rather young and of a different political mold than some of the older generation of Eritreans he knew. For that matter, our government did not have any practical experience in the administration of a federal state either. It was a whole new ball game for Ethiopians and Eritreans alike.

His appointment confirmed, *Ras* Andargachew arrived in Asmara some days before the take-over of the territory from the British Military Administration in 1952. The ceremony was very touching, starting first with a British military contingent that paraded with a military band, sounding a retreat march while the British Flag was lowered. Then the Ethiopian Flag was raised, and an Ethiopian army battalion followed with a military band playing our national hymn. It was a solemn and highly moving moment. I cannot describe the emotions that engulfed us; we all had tears in our eyes.

Once the handover was settled, we started preparing feverishly for the arrival of the Emperor in Eritrea, which was to take place on the first day of Ethiopian New Year 1945 (Ethiopian *(Julian)* Calendar). The program for his arrival was that he would cross the Mereb River by road where a ceremony would be held consecrating the return of Eritrea to the motherland. A plethora of dignitaries and high officials from all over the country had gathered in Adwa days before the event. Foreign Minister Aklilou, Professor John Spencer and I flew to Adwa the day before. I don't believe that the town had seen a gathering of so many dignitaries since Emperor Menelik's victory there. After a brief ribbon-cutting ceremony at the bridge across the Mereb River that separates the two territories, the Emperor and his retinue proceeded by road to Asmara. All along the road, a jubilant population greeted the Emperor.

A big reception was prepared in Asmara, followed a few days later by a visit to Massawa.

The Emperor's visit over, *Ras* Andargachew started his functions. I briefed him in detail about what had been done in setting up the federal structure and introduced him to the various officials that were heading the federal departments. He had already met with Tedla Bairu (later *Dejazmach*) and the Eritrean high officials. His working experience having been in the central government in Addis Ababa and the provincial administration in Harar, I sensed that he was not comfortable with this new type of governance where his powers were limited to that of the federal functions, while the local administration was independent and self-governing. Unlike Ethiopia, where the regular provincial administration had still to be reorganized, Eritrea had been under a modern system during the sixty years of Italian colonial rule and later for ten years under British Military Administration. In addition, the presence of a large foreign community dominated the economy of the territory. This was a new game that the *Ras* found difficult to adapt to. He was also badly influenced by some of the Eritrean political factions from the Akele Guzay and Serae clans who were challenging Tedla Bairu (who was a Hamassien) and his administration. In the meantime, Asfaha Wolde Mikael, who was also from Akele Guzay, had replaced Amde-Mikael Dessalegn as principal head of the Liaison Office which had been integrated with the federal administration. That made him de-facto Deputy to the Federal Representative. Most members of the Unionist Party, especially those residing in Ethiopia, were for immediate reunification. Many of them were well established within Ethiopia, some reaching the highest ranks in government and others successful in professional and business ventures. All these people, including the members of the Unionist Party in Eritrea, had a vested interest in the immediate union of Eritrea with Ethiopia. *Ato* Amde-Mikael and I shared the view that one should proceed with the unification as soon as possible before the consolidation of the federal system could create further problems because of the many contentious divisions in the Eritrean political context.

~

Personally, I could also foresee brewing problems emerging from the power-sharing between the federal and the local administrations. *Ras* Andargachew thought that he had the prerogative to intervene in Eritrean domestic affairs, while the Eritrean administration, defending its turf, did not agree to such interference. Eritrean internal politics also played a part in inflaming and exacerbating the contentions between some influential Addis Ababa-based Eritreans, who made the Federation an instrument for their own advancement. Actually, the federal statutes had clearly defined the role of the two authorities. Problems that occasionally arose could have been resolved easily with some goodwill and some appropriate decisions from the central government. Unfortunately, Addis Ababa chose not to interfere, preferring the usual smug equivocation and lack of clarity. On the Eritrean side, Tedla Bairu had his own problems with growing opposition to his leadership by the other Eritrean political and clan factions, mostly because of his authoritarian behavior, as well as the fact that he belonged to the Hamassein clan, and was a Protestant. Tedla was more of an intellectual than a politician. An honest and straightforward man, he was a school teacher by profession, hastily trained by the British military administration as district administrator. He had little political experience and no taste for the infighting and backbiting that was going on between the Eritrean political factions.

Two years later, Tedla Bairu resigned and was replaced as Chief Executive by Asfaha Wolde-Mikael who was from Akele Guzay and a much shrewder politician. He intimately knew the character and workings of the Ethiopian establishment. Asfaha, who was later bestowed with the high honorific title of *Bitwoded*, and appointed Minister of Justice, had worked for many years as an interpreter for General Nasi, Vice Governor-General of Italian East Africa. After the Liberation, *Bitwoded* Asfaha joined the Ethiopian provincial administration in Dessie, and with the increasing interest in Eritrea was appointed as Director in our Foreign Ministry. He was very active in the Unionist Party, especially within the pro-union Eritrean community in Addis Ababa. In later years, the Ethiopian Government was blamed for unilaterally abrogating the Federation. That was partly true because the Federation was in fact forced on us by the United Nations and was not of our volition. However, it was also true that many Eritreans and members of the Unionist party had actively supported the replacement of the federal status with a full union.

Although I was asked to continue working in Eritrea, I declined, and rejoined my post at the Ministry. On that occasion, the Emperor was kind enough to allow me the use of his personal airplane, a De-Havilland Dove which was a gift from the British Queen, to bring back my family from Asmara.

CHAPTER 14

Revising the Constitution

~

ONE OF THE PROVISIONS OF the UN resolution was to draft a democratic constitution for Eritrea. In light of this proposed new federal constitution, it became evident that a revision of the 1931 Ethiopian Constitution was necessary as well. This was particularly so since most of the objections of the international community to Ethiopia's claim to Eritrea derived from the fact that our regime was deemed autocratic and did not allow any democratic rights. A special Committee to revise the Ethiopian Constitution was formed under the Chairmanship of then Prime Minister, *Ras Bitwoded* Makonnen Endalkachew. Other members were *Ras* Abebe Aregay, *Tsehafi-Taezaz* Wolde-Giorgis Wolde-Yohannes, *Ato* Makonnen Habte-Wold, *Ato* Aklilou Habte-Wold, *Lij* Yilma Deressa and *Blatta* Zewde Belayneh. In addition to my duties as Chief of Protocol and head of the European Division, I was appointed Secretary of this committee. The function of the Committee was to examine the various drafts and suggestions that were received from various sources and make recommendations. It was tedious work because suggestions were coming from many sources. John H. Spencer, Principal Adviser to the Ministry of Foreign Affairs, Professor A.H. Garretson, Viverca (a former Czech Foreign Minister), and several other foreign advisers were also working on various drafts. I had to translate some of these into Amharic or explain their content verbally. It was a voluminous work. However, this was not the main problem. It was always difficult to hold a meeting because the Prime Minister and the other Ministers were very busy. Ultimately, it seemed to me that none were eager to recommend any amendment to the Constitution and assume the responsibility for it.

On one occasion I was sent to see His Highness *Ras* Kassa Hailu, who headed the Crown Council, whom my elders were reluctant to confront, and explain to him why some terms of the Constitution had to be amended. I explained that the changes were due to the new federal status of the country which necessitated some adjustments to our own constitution and that this was an understanding with the UN as the world body had approved the Federation. Having heard my account with attention, the *Ras* said: "Tell them to make it like the British Constitution." When I answered that there was not a single constitution in England but a series of Acts, he was shocked, I think that he thought I was fooling him, and he asked: "Where were you educated?" I replied that I was educated in Teferi Makonnen School and that I have no academic education, but that I had read something about the British political system. Upon this he told me to come back the day after, and that he would give his answer then. When I went to see him at the appointed time, the *Ras* received me most courteously and invited me for lunch, and said that being relatives, I should visit him more often. He obviously had inquired about what I had told him. As to the revision of the Constitution, he said that he had no objections in principle: "Tell them that they can do what they like." Then addressing me directly he told me, "Don't waste your time on this affair; in any case, whatever changes are made will never be implemented." When I reported that *Ras* Kassa had said that "They can make any change they want," the Emperor commented, "He is too conservative." In my mind, I wondered who of the two was more conservative.

For instance, during the revision of the Constitution, a suggestion came from one of the foreign advisers that the term "Elect of God" be taken out from the titles of the Emperor. As none of the members of the committee wanted to raise the issue with the Emperor, as secretary it seemed that the task was mine, and I was ordered to do it. When I reported the matter to the Emperor, he said quietly "Were it not for the will of God, how do you think that I came to this position?" and he truly meant it. Thus, I realized that all Ethiopian monarchies had existed in the absolute belief of their rights and duties inherited from history or myths, which they considered as a sacred trust and their manifest destiny. Axum, Roha, Lalibela, Gondar, the monasteries, churches and archeological sites we see today; the literature, laws, and social canons all derive from and were inspired by Biblical times. Obviously, the personality of Emperor Haile Selassie and that of his predecessors was also molded by this absolute faith.

~

A couple of weeks later the Emperor asked me what progress had been made by the Committee; I said that not much had been done of late because it was difficult to get all the members to meet, as they seemed to be busy with other matters. Then I asked if I could pose a question, and when he acquiesced, I asked: "Does Your Majesty really want the constitution to be revised?" He answered, "Yes, that is definitely our intention." "Then may I suggest that the Committee be appointed officially by Imperial Charter and this be proclaimed in the *Negarit Gazeta* (Official Bulletin). This way the responsibility of the committee will be clearly established, and all doubts that Your Majesty has no real desire to revise the constitution will cease." The Emperor responded, "It is a good idea. Present it to the Committee and tell them that we have agreed with it". After that I called the Committee, telling them that I had some new instructions from H.I.M. This time they all came, and I told them that the Emperor had agreed for the Committee to be appointed officially for the revision of the Constitution. My announcement caused considerable consternation. To my surprise, the first to protest against the idea was *Lij* Yilma Deressa, who said that this would create all sorts of difficulties for the workings of the Committee because once this was officially announced there would be a flood of suggestions and inquiries that would hamper its work. For the first time, the Committee agreed unanimously on an issue. When I reported their objection, the Emperor simply smiled. Obviously, *Lij* Yilma had a better perception of Ethiopian politics than I.

By that time, I was very frustrated. I had hoped that however minimal, a new liberalization of our politics would have occurred. After all, we had promised to the UN body that we would bring our Constitution in line with the Eritrean local constitution that contained the basic tenets of a democratic system of government. But nothing of the sort happened; it took three more years for the promulgation of the 1955 revised Constitution. Later, Prime Minister Aklilou Habte-Wold took pride in devising a way of circumventing some of the liberal conditions by adding to the articles "according to the law," without defining which law, and without providing a time-frame for the promulgation. The main opposition to a serious revision came from what one would call the "modern" elements of the Committee like Wolde-Giorgis, Aklilou and Makonnen Habte-Wold, rather than from the elder group of *Ras Bitwoded* Makonnen Endalkachew (then Prime Minister), *Ras* Abebe and Zewde Belayneh and even *Ras* Kassa, who smugly knew that the Emperor had no intention of relinquishing any power.

A great controversy occurred over the elections of the two Chambers of Parliament. The modern bureaucrat committee members insisted that the members of the Chamber of Deputies be elected by popular vote and that those of the Senate be appointed by the Emperor. The elder members of the Committee, *Ras-Bitwoded* Makonnen Endalkachew, *Ras* Abebe Aregay and *Blatta* Zewde Belayneh, took the position that dividing the parliament into two (one faction popularly elected and the other by Imperial appointment) would be likely to create future confrontations, and that as the Emperor is Father to all the people of the nation, both Chambers should be elected by popular vote. *Tsehafi-Taezaz* Wolde-Giorgis strongly opposed the idea. With regard to women's equal rights in all aspects of the Constitution, however, there was not a single controversy. I believe that if the Committee had presented the Emperor with a set of commonly agreed recommendations, he would probably have accepted them. But unfortunately, the power struggle amongst the various factions came into play. None of them were for a real democratic liberalization; all they cared for was for their personal position. Even some of the educated ones who had returned home and taken junior positions in government showed little interest in reforms; their interest was in advancing their own careers by joining one group or the other.

As to the power groups that consolidated on the political scene, *Tsehafi-Taezaz* Wolde-Giorgis, as Minister of the Pen and former Minister of Interior, was the virtual Prime Minister. All Imperial orders went through his office, therefore, he controlled all appointments of government officials. *Ato* Makonnen Habte-Wold having been at various times Minister of Commerce and Industry, Minister of Finance, Minister of Information, and Patron-Chairman of the Patriotic Association, the most important civic association in the country, controlled a large segment of the political and commercial community as well as the only media. In addition, Foreign Affairs also came under his sphere of influence, Aklilou Habte-Wold being his brother and a protégé of Wolde-Giorgis.

In the domestic political set-up, genuine liberal intellectuals such as Dr. Aleme-Work, Mesfin Zelleke, Getachew Zewge, Ashebir Gabre-Hiwot, Worku Gobena, Professor Tamrat and many others were excluded from any role in government right from the beginning because of their reformist views. Others, such as Makonnen Desta, Getahun

Tessema, Sereke-Brahan, Gashaw Zelleke who were already in government were accused of some vague fault or another and sent abroad or given demotions. The method of ostracizing people was to accuse them of some sort of misconduct, and keep them in suspense for years, more often than not without pay, if their properties were not arbitrarily seized. There was no legal court to appeal to; the best one could do was to find someone to intercede with the Emperor. This was, however, a difficult task, because once it was known that you were in disfavor with the Palace, most of your friends, and even your close relatives, would shun you. You became a social pariah. Officially you were free, but anything you tried to do was circumvented and made difficult. You were in a Kafkaesque realm. You went to the Palace every day and paid homage to the Emperor (a practice known as *dej tenat*), which served more to control your presence than to help solve your problems. Otherwise, provided you kept away from politics, life was quiet, pleasurable and peaceful.

Personally, my political views had matured and in many ways had radically changed. I have no formal education. My education, if any, derived from the varied exposures I had from the many currents of ideas and events I experienced. Extensive reading and social interactions with many cultures and societies had enlightened me and given me new perspectives on our society and politics. I was disenchanted with the way important matters of national significance were decided with little concern for the future - particularly concerning political reforms over which we had been criticized extensively in the UN. The limited reforms that were made consisted of an atrophied and badly implemented federal formula that brought little benefit to either the Ethiopian or Eritreans people. The urge for reforms of our own political system prompted by our exposure to critical world opinion had cooled down, and the usual paradigm of court politics and decision-making had set in.

CHAPTER 15

Paris

~

AT THIS POINT, BECAUSE OF my wife's health and her need for special-ized medical treatment, I asked to be posted abroad. As our Ambassador to France, *Fitawrari* Tafesse Habte-Mikael, was to return home shortly, I was appointed as Chargé d'Affaires at our Embassy in Paris. Paris was an ideal post for me as I knew the country and the culture well. Having worked on the Ethiopia-Djibouti frontier delimitation negotiations, I had received the honorific medal of *Officier de la Légion d'honneur* (the French order for military and civil merits). Moreover, I had several per-sonal friends in Paris with whom I had kept in contact throughout the years. The Embassy staff were people I knew well, and we were friends. There was the Commercial Attaché, Mr. Jean Ouannou whom I met during my earlier stay in Paris and my friend, Mr. Jean Lessay, the Press Attaché whom I have also mentioned. *Ato* Tekle-Tsadik Mekuria, First Secretary, from whom I took over, returned home shortly afterward.

The Embassy was situated in a very nice area near the Trocadéro on Avenue Georges Mandel. The building dated from around the turn of the 19th century. It was a baronial mansion, built mostly for social en-tertainment, with two large reception rooms, the owners' living apart-ments and many facilities like kitchens and servant quarters. It had been purchased in 1946 by *Ato* Tesfaye Tegegn, our first Ambassador to France after World War II. The building which had been abandoned by the owners sometime before the war was in very bad condition and needed a lot of repairs and some conversions to make it usable for an Embassy, particularly as it was to serve both as a residence and an office. Several appraisals and estimates were obtained by my predecessors to repair and refurbish the building, and proposals had been sent to our government, but no decision had been made. In the meantime, the estimated costs doubled while the deterioration of the building worsened. When I arrived in Paris in the summer of 1952, the building was utterly dysfunctional. We had some second-hand office furniture, no carpets of any kind except for an old rug in the office of the head of mission. We couldn't receive any serious visitors. People who came for visas or other business could not believe an Embassy could be in such poor condition. Some could not help exclaiming "*Ça alors*! Is this really the Embassy of Ethiopia?" It was very humiliating. Fortunately, *Fitawrari* Tafesse Habte-Mikael had rented a nice house in Villa Said, a cul-de-sac off Avenue Foch that served as a temporary residence, so I used it every time I had to receive an official or an Ambassador. The heating system in the Embassy did not work; when winter arrived the water pipes froze and burst, and some rooms were flooded. It became absolutely necessary to refurbish the place. I had an up-to-date appraisal made, the cost of which turned out to be much higher than those made previously. I reported the matter to Prime Minister Aklilou, then Foreign Minister, who saw the condition of the building himself while he was vacationing in France. He and his wife stayed with us at the residence for about three weeks. I suggested that if we could not afford the expenses necessary to repair the building, we should sell it and buy another one in good condition. I made him visit several other buildings in prime locations which we could buy. He agreed and told me to report the matter to Addis Ababa, which meant to the Emperor, for a final decision. After some hesitation, my proposal to sell the old building and get another one that did not require much expenditure was approved.

We put the old building up for sale and started looking for a suitable new place for our Embassy. The sale of our building at the appraised price turned out to be difficult because of the amount of money needed for the extensive renovations that were required. Fortunately, having heard that we were trying to sell, our immediate neighbors – some Catholic nuns who ran a private school - offered to buy the building because they wanted to enlarge their facility. Finding another building in a suitable area did not prove to be easy, especially within the limits of the selling price of the old building, since we knew that our government would not authorize any additional funds. Together with some engineers, I visited over forty buildings in central Paris. None were suitable for our purpose, or were too expensive and did not meet our financial limits. Luckily my good connections with French society served me well; an opportunity arose because the friend of a friend of mine inherited from an aunt the building where the Embassy is situated to this day. He wanted to sell it because of the high taxation involved if he were to keep it as personal property. I visited the building, which was in fair condition. Although it was built as a private residence, it had plenty of space to accommodate our needs; that is the residence and the offices, including the possibility of obtaining a permit to build an additional floor when needed. Situated along the Champs de Mars on one side and Avenue Charles Floquet on the other, next to the Eiffel Tower, it was a prime property in one of the most prestigious quarters of Paris.

The asking price for the property was about thirty-five million French francs, while we were offered some forty-five million francs for the old building. Thus I proposed that we go ahead with the sale and buy this one, which would leave us some ten million francs for repairs and refurbishing. My suggestion was approved, and I proceeded to do so. Once the new building had been renovated and the offices transferred, the new Ambassador to France, *Blatten-Geta* Ephrem Tewolde-Medhin, moved from the rented residence to the new premises. A few months later, when the Emperor made on an official visit to France, the state dinner and reception for the French President were held in our new Embassy.

~

In early 1954, the Emperor was to visit the United States. The complicated itinerary that had been arranged - God knows by whom- was for him to fly to Paris by a US government plane and then transfer by road to Le Havre, where he would board the SS United States. On his return, he would come again to France where he would rest for a week before proceeding to Yugoslavia on an official visit. There was some commotion during the trip because the plane transporting the Emperor experienced engine trouble about one hour away from Paris. Eventually, everything turned out all right. During his one-week stay, we drove His Majesty from Paris to Rouen to dine at a famous restaurant. The Emperor was so pleased with the meal that he gave a gold medal to the owner. The final problem arose in Le Havre when it was discovered that the Emperor's chief of intelligence, Major Workneh Gebeyehu, did not have any passport or identification papers, and the captain of the ship refused to take him on board. When asked why he did not bring any travel documents, he answered that traveling with the Emperor he thought that he would not need any. So much for the reputed high intelligence of the head of Ethiopian security! I couldn't find the American Consul in Le Havre; he was off for the weekend and the same for officials at the US Embassy in Paris. I called the State Department in Washington, and after many consultations, they agreed to let him on board if I gave him some type of identity paper. I don't want to dwell on all the tribulations I went through, but it was a most annoying episode.

According to plan, the Emperor was to proceed to Yugoslavia upon his return from America. The program was that he would take a week-long rest in the South of France and proceed from there to Belgrade. We had to arrange lodging, transportation and site visits for him and the accompanying officials. I had made reservations for the Emperor and his close staff at the Eden Roc Hotel in Antibes, and for the rest of his party in one of the major hotels in Nice, where I also booked an alternative suite for the Emperor. Given a choice, the senior members decided that the Emperor should stay in the same hotel with them, so I canceled the reservation at Eden Roc. The next day when the Emperor wanted to go on his usual walk, the lobby of the hotel was so packed with journalists, paparazzi and all sorts of curious people that he could hardly go out of the hotel, let alone take a walk in the street. He called me and said he wanted to go back to the Eden Roc Hotel, where I managed to get three single rooms, despite my previous cancellation.

Nothing special happened during the few days in the south of France, I am merely mentioning the event because it was the first and the last occasion I was ever close person-to-person with the Emperor for an extended time. Since all his entourage was staying in Nice, most of the time I was alone with him. He was dapper and very organized. When I went to his room, everything was orderly and in place. He did not talk much but asked many questions about France and Europe. I did my best to answer honestly and clearly to his questions, especially about our relations with the various countries. I told him frankly that some reforms were necessary for our system of government if we wanted to benefit from our relations with the western democratic countries. He listened but did not comment, which left me with some optimism. Although his general behavior was quite simple - almost modest - his personality emanated a tremendous aura and great dignity. He had an enchanting smile and was very charming and amiable to people. Foreigners of all sorts warmed up to him very easily. Nevertheless, one could discern, underlying his gentle appearance, a very resolute personality, highly conscious of his powers and prerogatives.

6. 1950, my wife Woizero Martha Nassibou with Mrs Eleanor Roosevelt and two Indonesian diplomats delegates to the UN Third Committee at a lunch offered by Mrs Roosevelt at her home in Hyde Park, New York

7. My first mission to Sweden as Chargé d'Affaires, photo with Imperial Ethiopian Airforce officers: Standing L-R Col. Mitiku Muleta, myself, Lt Gen. Assefa Ayene, Engineer ....., Count Carl Gustaf von Rosen. Seated L-R, Lt. Michael Sahlemariam, Col. Getachew Brig. Gen. Markorios Haile, Col. Gadissa Guma

8. *Ready for a State Function: L-R, Tsehafi-Taezaz Tefera Work, General Makonnen Deneke, Ras Mesfin Sileshi, Tsehafi-Taezaz Wolde Giorgis and me*

9. *1948, Asmara, Eritrea with Prime Minister Aklilou*

10. *The Emperor's State visit to Germany 1954.*
Source German Federal Archives

11. *The Emperor with German President Theodore*
Heuss, 1954. Source German Federal Archives

CHAPTER 16

Bonn

~

BLATTEN-GETA EPHREM TEWOLDE-MEDHIN HAVING TAKEN up his appointment as Ambassador to Paris, I was appointed to the German Federal Republic as Minister Extraordinary & Plenipotentiary. It was the first permanent diplomatic mission Ethiopia was establishing in Germany. It was a very hectic time for me. After having presented my credentials in Germany, I continued running back and forth between Bonn and Paris, trying to finish the Embassy work in Paris because of the Emperor's imminent state visit there that would be followed by visits to Belgium, Holland, Germany, the Scandinavian countries and lastly Switzerland.

In Germany, even nine years after World War II had ended, not all the debris left from the war had been removed yet, and reconstruction was still proceeding. Housing was difficult to find in Bonn which had become the temporary capital of the country in 1949. After some searching, we found a villa in Roisdorf, a small village on the outskirts, and some office space in Bonn itself. The Emperor's visit to the German Federal Republic went very well; the German government did not spare any effort to make the visit successful. As the first visit to Germany by a Head of State of a foreign country after the war, it was seen as an affirmation of German sovereignty, as the country at that time was still ruled by the Four Powers. The program was quite extensive and consisted of visits to some of the major manufacturing and agricultural industries. Besides the official receptions and functions, an important event was a luncheon Mr. Alfred Krupp, the German industrialist, gave for the Emperor at the Villa Hugel, the Krupp family estate. He had invited several hundred leaders of German industry from all over the country. It was a magnificent and grandiose function, befitting the Krupp legacy, and a sort of demonstration that German industry was still powerful and being revitalized after the disastrous outcome of the war. I heard later that the German Government was hesitant to include the Krupp invitation in the program because of his case at the Nuremberg trials. However, he eventually won the argument and his reception was included in the official functions. Despite his condemnation by the victorious Allies, he was obviously highly respected, popular, and unquestionably the leader of German industry.

At the end of the luncheon, Krupp asked the Emperor for a private conference with some of the senior industrial leaders and invited him to a separate conference room. Strangely enough, the Emperor decided to go to the meeting without any other members of his retinue, except for me as an interpreter. About twenty heads of major industries attended the meeting. They all stated their desire to assist Ethiopia, and the meeting ended by setting up an Ethio-German Commission to pursue the matter further. This outcome put me in a difficult position because some of the Ethiopian ministers resented being excluded from the meeting, as well as my being the sole person privy to supposedly important secrets that might have been discussed. Another incident had happened earlier, at the banquet given by the Emperor for the German President. Our Foreign Minister, Aklilou Habte-Wold (my direct superior), called me and said that according to European protocol a Foreign Minister took precedence over a Minister of the Pen and that he should be seated higher at the table, in place of *Tsehafi- Taezaz* Wolde-Giorgis. His assertion placed me in a delicate situation because I had nothing to do with Court protocol which was the responsibility of the Emperor's *Aide-de-Camp*. When I told the ADC, he told me that the minister should know his rank, and refused the request. Actually, I was a bit surprised at Aklilou's request, because I knew that Wolde-Giorgis had been his promoter and supporter throughout his career and that coming from the same background in Bulga district in Showa, they were close friends. In fact, at that time *Ato* Makonnen Habte-Wold, the elder brother of Aklilou, and Wolde-Giorgis were close allies and the most powerful officials of the government. Obviously, a rift had occurred between the two high officials.

Wherever he went, the Emperor was received by huge crowds. As a matter of fact, Ethiopia was well known in Germany, particularly in religious and academic circles as relations between the two countries spanned more than five centuries. Moreover, the myth of a Christian Kingdom known as the country of Prester John, later identified with Ethiopia, was a popular story in Europe dating from the 12th century. The legend of the Queen of Sheba had also inspired many poetical and literary works. Scholars had conducted serious research on Ethiopia; an *Historia Aethiopica* had been written by Hiob Ludolf, a German orientalist and Ethiopic scholar, in 1681. Since then, missionaries and scientists had frequently visited Ethiopia and played a major role in establishing Ethiopian Studies in Germany. Thus the Emperor's visit had an aura of a legendary pageant - probably very different from what the public expected to see. The elegance and dignity of the visitors, the gold and glitter of the uniforms and decorations, the Sabean beauty of H.I.H. Princess Sara Gizaw, Duchess of Harar, were very impressive and gave the occasion a festive mood, such as most likely had not been seen for a long time. From Germany, the Emperor proceeded on an official visit to the Scandinavian countries, after which he was to end his European tour in Switzerland, where again I was tasked to make the arrangements.

The visit went to Switzerland well and according to the program. Aside from the official functions, Mr. Bührle, the owner of the Oerlikon arms manufacturing complex, who was Ethiopian Honorary Consul, gave a luncheon for the Emperor and the imperial family. Bührle had been a strong supporter of Ethiopia during the Italian invasion. Despite the arms embargo imposed on Ethiopia, he had managed to smuggle in some anti-aircraft guns and other armaments that were hidden under false truck bodies. Before the invasion, a few officers of the Imperial Guard had also received training in his establishment. While we were in Zurich, on one occasion, I went to *Teshafi-Taezaz* Tefera-Work's room for some inquiry, where I found Wolde-Giorgis and Aklilou arguing over who united Eritrea with Ethiopia, both claiming the success as their own personal achievement. When Aklilou saw me, he called me and said that I could tell the truth, because I had been fully involved in the issue right from the beginning. This again put me on the spot caught between two powerful ministers, although it was true that they both had had their role - Aklilou on the foreign stage, and Wolde-Giorgis on the domestic scene. Miffed by their arrogant pretensions, I answered by asking, "What about the thousands of people who worked for the Union? What about those who died and suffered for it? It is true that you two were overseeing the proceedings, but it is the effort of many people that brought the unity!" Unfortunately, it was not the answer either had wanted to hear. Wolde-Giorgis was openly angry, and he threatened me with some words like 'I will show you.' Although I did not have much to do with internal politics, I sensed that some serious rift had developed between the two whom I had known to be very strong allies and that I had probably unknowingly fallen into disfavor with both, especially Aklilou who was my direct boss. It didn't take me long to find out.

∽

The Emperor's state visit was a good omen for my mission in Germany. Our embassy became very popular amongst the German political circles and the diplomatic corps. My wife, *Woizero* Martha Nassibou, who as I mentioned had attended the New York Arts Students League in the US and the Beaux Arts Academy in Paris, was a great asset to the mission. In a matter which was later to become an issue while I was still in Paris, I had been ordered to find an interior decorator for the new Jubilee Palace that was being built in the capital, and I had asked a friend, the Editor of "*Connaissance des Arts*", a well-known art magazine, to help me with this. So the designers prepared a proposal which I forwarded to Addis Ababa. Our Embassy in London had also sent a proposal from Asprey's, a famous decorator. In the meantime, without my knowledge, the Minister of Public Works, *Lij* Araya Abebe, had signed a contract with a German furniture manufacturer in Düsseldorf to furnish the new Palace. It also appeared that the Private Secretary of the Emperor had approved the German's presentation. Having learned this, I declined to be further involved in this matter although I had been asked to follow up. In my view, the style chosen was typical for a hotel lobby and not suitable for an Imperial Palace.

The Emperor's visit to Germany was followed by a visit to Ethiopia by the German Minister of Economics, Herr Ludwig Erhard, (responsible for what would be called the "German Economic Miracle" and future Chancellor) whom I escorted to Addis Ababa in the summer of 1955. At that time Germany was just coming into the world scene after the end of the Allied Occupation. By making a state visit to West Germany in 1954, the Emperor had created a lot of goodwill towards our country. The Germans were willing to extend all their assistance for our development, and even make it a showcase of their foreign aid program. It was also a new positive role that post-war Germany could play on the international scene. Unfortunately, for lack of preparation on our side, we did not use this chance that could have brought a substantial input to our economic development. The German Minister was staying only three days. On the last day of his visit - I think it was a Saturday morning - Haddis Alemayehu and I were called and asked to prepare a memorandum about the visit and its conclusions. Since we had neither participated in any of the discussions nor had been informed about the proceedings, we were both surprised and angry, so we wrote a very general and empty statement about the excellent relations between the two countries fostered by the Minister's visit. The Minister's visit was concluded with the establishment of an Ethio-German committee to work further on the collaboration between the two countries. There was a lot of goodwill from the German side to help Ethiopia develop its economy in a substantial manner, and it would have been an excellent opportunity in those days when foreign aid was rather limited. Unfortunately, it turned out our government had no intention of developing projects of economic scale with Germany, except for some social health projects. In addition to the general apathy and self-fulfilling indolence of our high officials, I also suspect that some colonial powers who were displeased with the presence of Germany, a rival colonial power, back in Africa, particularly through Ethiopia, may have exerted influence accordingly

~~

The official visit of the German Minister over, I stayed longer to pursue a few projects I had presented to the government. The first project was to make a feature film on the Ethiopian patriotic resistance; the second was to have foreign banks open branches in Ethiopia and to make the *birr* a convertible currency, both of which would have attracted the foreign investments we badly needed for our development. The third project was to give some impetus to the Krupp group that had already opened an office in Addis Ababa, managed by one of their top executives. I had come to learn that the Krupp representative was seem-ingly getting little response from our authorities.

As customary, a committee of people who hadn't a clue about film-making was appointed to review and approve the matter of the proposed film. I had presented a fully prepared script and a financial estimate to be committed by a producer that I had already found. Thus the project could have been achieved at no cost to our government, except for some goodwill and cooperation. The only person who supported the project was *Ato* Kebede Mikael, a very well known author and Director of the National Library. The committee managed to muddle the matter and passed it on to the Ministry of Information that was headed then by *Ato* Makonnen Habte-Wold. *Ato* Makonnen was frank and told me that a movie about the patriotic resistance was not of great urgency at the time and that if I made a film about the Emperor he would give me all the money I needed. This was difficult for me because the subject of my project was the Resistance inside Ethiopia during the occupation while the Emperor was in exile abroad - a completely different subject. Apart from that, I had personally borrowed twenty-five thousand dollars to prepare the movie, which I would have gotten back from the producer once the project was approved. Deeply disappointed, I said that I would think about it, and dropped the matter. I did not want to get involved in making a documentary about the Emperor, which could involve me in some unwanted complications.

Regarding the banking project, another committee was appoint-ed, which concluded that Ethiopia had money of its own and did not need any foreign investors - a notion born out of fear that an active foreign role in the economy might diminish the extent of government control. There was an underlying governing perception - that has re-tarded the development of the country - that I should have considered in my proposals. The Ethiopian adage that describes it best is *"Sew kekebere bekelalu ayigezam,"* which means, "If people acquire wealth, they will not be easy to govern" - a convenient policy for all dictators, be they monarchs or revolutionaries. As for the Krupp project, this was relegated to the Private Secretary of the Emperor, who told me that he was very busy and would attend to it as soon as he could. Profoundly disillusioned, I returned to my post in Bonn.

CHAPTER 17

Power Struggles

⁓

AT THIS POINT, I REALIZED that I had made some mistakes. I had forgotten the power struggle between the Patriots' faction and the Exiles that included the Emperor himself. Eventually, the Exiles had won and now held power, while the Patriots, except for a few such as *Ras* Abebe Aregay, were relegated to provincial posts or retired, actually excluding them from the center of power. A movie dedicated to the heroism of the Patriots would have rejuvenated the image of this faction, who were very unhappy because they did not get the positions they thought their service deserved. The Emperor had a tight grip on every part of the government and had reverted to the customary form of traditional court rule, which was hardly adequate for a country that had changed profoundly during the occupation. While they were in exile, changes that he and his close advisers did not reckon with had taken place in the governing system. Their terms of reference for the governance of the country were still anchored in the past, both in thought and in deed. Furthermore, by the time I was trying to push my projects, the internal political landscape had also changed: the rift between the Makonnen HabteWold-Aklilou faction and Wolde-Giorgis had come out into the open, and the latter seemed to be losing ground. All sorts of rumors were being spread about Wolde-Giorgis' eventual demise. Unfortunately for him, with his perceived arrogance and sometimes excessive aggressiveness, he had made many more enemies than friends, so there was little sympathy or support for him from any side.

Also, I was having problems with my own situation. Colleagues at the Foreign Office had warned me that there were concerns - to which I hadn't paid much attention - about my close friendship with some students with radical ideas, and regarding my exuberant lifestyle. Girmame Neway, a cousin, and some other students had stayed with me while passing through Paris on their return home. In Germany, I had also hosted many students, some of them members of the Imperial family. Indeed, our social life in Germany was very active; we were very popular with German society and the diplomatic corps. Friends from various countries came to visit us often. I suspect that this created some envy on the part of some Embassy staff in Paris and Bonn. As usual, some were spying on others and had reported all sorts of false accusations to Addis about the purchase of the new Embassy in Paris, and goodness knows what else.

First, *Dejazmach* Zewde Gabre-Selassie was sent to Paris to investigate if there had been some financial misconduct in the sale of the former embassy and the acquisition of the new one. I have never known what he reported. In fact, there was nothing to report, apart from an additional ten thousand dollars paid to renew the lift. Otherwise, the new embassy building was purchased, refurbished and furnished out of the proceeds from the sale of the old building. Then came an order to investigate two students, sons of *Ato* Wolde-Giorgis Wolde-Yohannes, a senior editor of Ethiopian newspapers (not to be confused with the government official of the same name). They were accused of being die-hard Communists. I did not know the intrigues behind it. Nevertheless, I hired a private investigator and cleared the young men of the absurd charges against them. Then a former member of the Imperial Guard was appointed to the embassy in Germany as a "student." Knowing that he was an agent sent to spy on us, I refused to accept him, saying that it was demoralizing for the regular personnel. If he was a student he should stay as such, and not pose as a member of the embassy staff, I maintained. The question of the furniture for the Jubilee Palace arose again, and I was ordered to follow up and take care of the matter. Again I replied that as I had no knowledge of the contract, the person who made the agreement should come and check if all the items were completed. In the end, *Lij* Araya came himself to Germany to handle the final details.

Meanwhile, the Wolde-Giorgis issue had climaxed, and he was sent away as Governor to Arussi. Some of his strong supporters were dealt with similarly, such as Lt.-General Abye Abebe who was named Ambassador to France, and a former patriot leader *Dejazmach* Tsehayou Inqo-Selassie who was appointed Minister of Health and sent to Germany to visit the pharmaceutical and health industry. These steps were a way of keeping them out of the country and prevent them from creating trouble. *Dejazmach* Tsehayou stayed in Germany for about a month, during which time I assigned a member of the Embassy to assist him.

At the same time, in Ethiopia life was good, Eritrea had returned to the Motherland, the country was politically stable, the Emperor's reputation as a wise elderly statesman was well established, and he was highly respected worldwide. Despite its slow growth, the economy was stable, and social life was gracious and fashionable. Typical of a royal court government, decision-making was extremely slow and influenced by the continuous in-fighting of the power factions. At that particular moment, the dominant affair was the preparations for the Jubilee Celebrations of the Emperor's Coronation – the 25th year of his reign. It gave birth to a lot of speculation as to what changes would be made in the government, and about who would receive the new nominations; whether the Crown Prince would be given more powers; what changes would be made to the revised Constitution, and so forth.

～

For us who were living abroad, all this was rather remote. It was manifested only by the lack of any response from the home office to our inquiries. Most diplomatic posts were filled by people considered undesirable by the power center and sent abroad to simmer comfortably in their frustration. I do not put myself in that category, as I was a very junior functionary, presumably on the rise. Besides the representative function, diplomatic missions were rarely used for more productive purposes. Both the Emperor and the Minister preferred dealing directly with the foreign missions in Addis Ababa. By the same token, people appointed to foreign posts were rarely up to the job, either professionally or culturally. This had it is own rationale since little was expected from them. A few years back, when *Lij* Membere Yayehirad was Vice Minister, *Ato* Haddis Alemayehu, the other Director Generals and myself had proposed a project to form career diplomatic officers. However, that proposal was never supported by then Foreign Minister Aklilou Habte-Wold.

As for our daily life in Germany, our social calendar was full. Because of the friends we had cultivated during our sojourn in Europe and America - my wife through her network of school friends, and I through my work - most high social circles in Europe were opened to us. I guess that this was duly reported to the Emperor by some of my staff and passing visitors, creating jealousy and disapproval in high places. At this point, I had lost my hope of achieving anything serious in terms of the mission.

CHAPTER 18

A Difficult Homecoming

~⁀

IN 1956, I WAS CALLED home for reasons that were not explained to me. For two months, I went every day to the Palace to pay my respects, but still, nobody was telling me why I had been recalled. My family was left alone in Germany, and I was very angry about my own dilemma and all the intrigues that were going on. Then one afternoon I was called to the Palace in the presence of the Emperor. He was in the Blue Room. I could see immediately that his attitude towards me had changed; he addressed me angrily and said that I was a thief. It had been falsely reported to him that there were some discrepancies in the Embassy's accounts. The monthly accounts of all diplomatic missions were sent by the diplomatic pouch and opened first at the Palace before forwarding to the Ministry. Utterly shocked and without much reflection, I said that I was not a thief and that anyway, what was there to steal? He asked, "What do you mean?" I responded, "Where is the money to steal? Even our pay is never on time; we survive on overdrafts. If I had wanted money, I would have looked for some other work." Not so much what I said, but the tone I took in replying made him angrier and I was dismissed. *Abba* Hanna, the Emperor's confessor, was standing by the door when I walked out. He caught me by the arm and told me that I shouldn't have answered as I did. He said that instead, I should have admitted my guilt and asked for the Emperor's forgiveness, and added that I had made a bad mistake.

When I went out, I immediately saw that everybody knew that I had fallen from grace. And let me tell you, when you were out of favor with the Emperor, you were out in the field on you own. Acquaintances disappeared, people you used to know avoided you, even some of your family dropped you. My mother was angry with me. Being a favorite cousin of the Emperor, and responsible for women affairs at the Palace, whatever the Emperor said was sacrosanct for her. I became a non-person, lost in a solitary desert. Despite the fact that my family was still in Germany during those months that I was in suspense waiting to know why I was called, my pay had been stopped. I had to scramble to bring back my family.

~

The following two years were mentally a very painful period in my life and a very taxing time for my family. I had no job and could not get into business or any another employment without being officially dismissed from government service, which I was not. We survived with some income that my wife and I had from our properties. I went almost every morning to the Palace to petition to the Emperor, a traditional practice known as *dej tenat* ("paying court from the outside") when one is in disgrace and seeking his pardon, or wanting to present a petition. It was a humiliating and demoralizing condition that was materially and morally debilitating, and especially for people who had no resources of their own because it could go on for years. Thus I joined the multitude of people who crowded the Palace soliciting some favor. Paradoxically, being at the Palace every day turned out to be an interesting position from which to scrutinize the politics of the country. This look at the politics from the outside was a revelation for me; working in Foreign Affairs, I had paid little mind to internal politics. Nor had I sought to join any of the family or regional-related groupings that were scurrying for power around the Palace. The Duke of Harar, Prince Makonnen, remained a good friend. He even helped me by giving me a consulting job in one of his business ventures from which I received a small emolument. We were estranged from my half-brother Mesfin because of family litigation over some land about which I didn't care, so I could not turn to him. The one happy and blessed event that brought my family joy and brightened our spirits during that otherwise gloomy period was the birth of my daughter Saba in Paris on Ethiopian Christmas day, January 7, 1958.

During that difficult time, my closest friends were Lt.-General Abye Abebe, General Samuel Beyene, General Mengistu Neway and Girmame Neway (all cousins and relatives), and *Dejazmach* Takele Wolde-Hawariat, whom I knew in my younger days when my father was Minister of Agriculture and he was the Director-General. He was also married to an aunt, *Woizero* Askale Wolde-Amanuel. The others were young intellectuals and professionals like Seyoum Sebhat, Habte-Ab Bairu, Belatchew Asrat, Alemseged Feqada-Selassie Hirouy and others with whom I shared many thoughts about the conditions of the country. As for my troubles, I also blamed myself for not having paid much more attention to domestic politics.

Eventually, I decided to follow the normal practice and I asked *Ras* Abebe Aregay to intercede for me with the Emperor so that I may be allowed to be relieved from government service and follow my personal ends. The request was permitted by the Emperor. Then I applied for an import license from the Ministry of Commerce and Industry where the Minister was *Kibur Ato* Makonnen Habte-Wold, to whom I owe a lot for the help he gave me throughout the years. He was a friend of my father, and I had worked with him on the Eritrean issue as a liaison between the Foreign Ministry and the Ministry of Information of which he was then the Minister. He was a very wise and responsible statesman by any definition. For example, on one occasion, the American Ambassador had complained that there was no response to some projects they had proposed, particularly a mobile "visual education" program that was to have been shown around the rural areas. A committee composed of the Ministries of Education, Interior, and Foreign Affairs was set up to look into the matter. After examining the project, we all supported it, except for *Ato* Makonnen, who said, "I agree in principle. However, have you considered the fact that we don't have the means to sustain such a program on the ground, which would create false expectations amongst the public, thus making the government a liar?" *Ato* Makonnen was also the creator of a whole new class of Ethiopian small businessmen, a field that was generally dominated by European, Arab, and Indian merchants. He established the Handicraft School from where traditional crafts like jewelry, weaving, carpet making and other local industries developed. An important cultural center that he established was the Patriotic Association - *YeAger Fiker Mehaber* - through which traditional music, literature, and theater were promoted. The Association also served as a central civic organization that promoted many communal activities. *Kibur Ato* Makonnen Habte-Wold was a humble and just man who was completely dedicated to service to the Nation.

Having obtained my business license, I borrowed 1,500 *birr* from my brother-in-law Berhanu Nassibou, bought some furniture, and opened an office in Arada district named "Imru Zelleke, Import Export Consultant Inc.". Having no capital to work with, I decided to start looking for representations of foreign companies interested in export to Ethiopia, and I approached the commercial sections of the various foreign missions in Addis. Thus I obtained the agencies of scores of companies, some of which had substantial business with Ethiopia. The best agencies I got were the cigarette manufacturers from the US and Britain: British American Tobacco Co. and Brown &Williamson Co.; as well as manufacturers producing synthetic fibers used by the cotton factories and weavers from France; and others from various countries. I also opened a business consulting and public relations service, "Promotional Arts, Ltd," doing advisory and publicity work. We produced an illustrated pamphlet with a map of Addis Ababa with historical sites and large roadside posters for Ethiopian Airlines. A third business that I set up was "Shebaland Tours, Ltd" as a tour operator before the Ethiopian Tourist Agency was established. I made arrangements with Kuoni, a large Swiss tour agency that organized weekly safari trips to East Africa, to include a one-day stop-over in Addis Ababa on their way to Kenya. The program consisted of a visit to the Palace, to some churches, the Mercato and an Ethiopian dinner at the Addis Ababa restaurant. It was a full-day event that the tourists liked and found of historical interest. While doing all this activity, I was also intensely involved in politics, which, however, badly affected my health.

CHAPTER 19

Modernity and Tradition Clash

~⁀

Here, I would like to talk briefly about the post-Liberation period in which a tremendous amount of work was done to secure the sovereignty of the nation and establish a normal government structure. It could be said that Ethiopian political development went through three main phases of change in the post-Liberation era.

The first phase covered the fifteen years following the liberation, 1941 – 1955. These were the most critical and most challenging for the Imperial Government, which had very limited trained manpower and scarce financial resources. Yet, it was a period of great achievements. What made it relatively easy was also the great character of the Ethiopian people, who always manage to retain order among themselves in moments of crisis, even when the institutions of the State are weakened or altogether absent. Getting rid of the British quasi-occupation and starting the internal institutions and structures of the State from scratch was no easy matter. The National Central Bank, the Commercial Bank and a whole range of government institutions were organized, such as Ethiopian Airlines, the Highway Authority, and the Telecommunications Authority. The *birr* was established as the national currency, the Penal, Civil and Commercial Codes were promulgated. The armed forces and the police were formed and trained, and law and order were established. Education was expanded, and hundreds of students were sent abroad. Internationally Ethiopia was playing her role as a fully-fledged member of the free world and a founding member of the United Nations, a signatory to Dumbarton Oaks, and a founding member of the World Bank and the International Monetary Fund. Ethiopian armed forces participated in the UN forces in the Korean War. Eritrea was reunited with the motherland. A revised Constitution was adopted in 1955. Ethiopia had proven to be a viable, responsible and dynamic member of the world community, with a promising future. Both the nation and her leadership enjoyed tremendous prestige and approval around the world.

The second phase started when, with the return of students to Ethiopia and the availability of trained personnel, the administration expanded, and a new class of professional cadre came on the political scene. The civil service was gradually improving with the integration of returning students, but unfortunately, most of them had degrees in liberal arts and had very little training or knowledge of practical subjects such as finance, economics, science, and administration. And very few had professional qualifications. For instance, I recall the case of a student who had graduated in organic chemistry for whom no position was found. Eventually, he was assigned to the ammunitions factory, about which he knew nothing, and finally was sent back for retraining in public health. As the demand for trained personnel was very high, promotions were very fast, and many former students sought to advance their careers rather than introduce innovations. A few adopted radical positions which put them at odds with the prevailing system.

By the late 1950s, the enthusiasm and drive that had stimulated the post-Liberation period had started to fade; a certain smugness and indulgence had set in. Basking in the limelight of the world scene, the leadership failed to pay enough attention to the growing demands at home arising from the socio-economic and political transformations that had occurred inside the country. While in exile, the experience acquired by the Emperor and the entourage that came to power after the Liberation focused on the diplomatic and political struggle they had continued in order to regain recognition and freedom for the country. Apart from their limited experience in modern administration, there was little in their political makeup that prepared them to manage the rapid changes that were transforming the country with the introduction of new programs and structures. Their prevailing outlook regarding governance of the country was still anchored in the era before the Italian Occupation. They could hardly understand the psychological and societal impact and the changes that the Occupation had brought to bear on Ethiopian society. Thus a tragic dichotomy began to take place. On one hand, the government took a progressive stand, introducing and establishing new institutions and new laws and regulations, while on the other hand it was dragging its feet in making serious reforms and implementing even those that it had promoted of its own volition such as land reform, the administration of the interior, freedom of expression, and democratization of the political system. Instead, it was adding more bureaucratic structures. A quinquennial social and economic plan were adopted, and the economy was stable. Yet, investments were slow and inadequate for the growing demand. For instance, credit was very limited, and foreign exchange strictly controlled. Mortgage financing was limited to three years with a one hundred percent collateral, severely restricting real estate and urban development. Only a few persons in power could enjoy such privileges. Commercial credit was also available to some well-established, mostly foreign, businesses. Apart from those engaged in traditional trade, it was extremely difficult for young Ethiopian entrepreneurs to start up a business. Despite a free market economic policy, getting a business license was also a discouraging, tedious and bureaucratic process. Foreign investments were few, and they were not actively sought - the suspicion of foreign elements continued to persist. Powerful driving personalities like *Tsehafi-Taezaz* Wolde-Giorgis, *Lij* Yilma Deressa, *Dejazmach* Kebede Tessema, *Dejazmach* Kifle Dadi, Major-General Mulugeta Buli and others had faded from the political center. Court politics and intrigues dominated public life; all decision-making was highly centralized in the Palace, which bogged down the workings of the State. Sycophancy, opportunism, and cronyism prevailed instead of statesmanship.

～

The third period culminated in 1960 with the attempted *coup d'état* by General Mengistu Neway and his brother Girmame. The tragic and vile mass murder by Girmame of unarmed elderly people assembled under the pretense that the Empress was gravely sick, marked a deep scar on the national conscience, introducing an ugly precedent that deeply marred traditional political values. The killing of a substantial number of leaders, whose views had a balancing role in the body politic, stifled any predisposition to change. Thus, a group whose opinion and advice weighed on the Emperor's decisions was eliminated from the political body, and an opportunity for some needed reforms was lost in spite of the progress made in the earlier years. The government did not learn anything from this tragic and violent occurrence and continued with its indolent pace until some reforms became inevitable. The government's response to the growing crisis was a meek nominal transfer of power to the Prime Minister. Thus the political firmament became dominated by Aklilou, his brother Akale-Work and some younger bureaucrats. However, the Prime Minister, of his own volition, had no organized office of his own through which to follow up the affairs of the country. He had only a few assistants in his office and nothing else. When I asked him how he could manage his functions of Prime Minister without an organization to back him up, he answered that he consulted directly with ministers when a particular issue arose.

Although they were occasionally consulted, the so-called conservative elements were limited to some high titled posts like the Crown Council with consultative functions, the Emperor making the final decisions. Hence, typical of court rule, those with close access to the Emperor had more influence than the Prime Minister and his Cabinet, even on major issues. With the return of graduate students from abroad, new political groupings had formed, and these were also divided into French, English and American educated factions. Due to the pressing need to modernize the administration, promotions to high government posts came relatively easy for the graduates. While this influx improved the central administration, it had little effect on the internal governance of the country, which was left mostly to inept political appointees or some discontented officials. There were hardly enough trained judges and administrators to implement the fairly sophisticated legal instruments and legislation that had been promulgated. Most development remained centered in the capital, with the provinces left to strive as best they could under mostly incompetent and abusive officials. During that time, the Emperor's attention focused on foreign relations. He visited the United States, most of the West European countries, and in 1959, he also visited the USSR.

That there was serious discontent in the provinces was evident. A serious cause of dissatisfaction amongst the vast number of the population was the justice system. Although a modern legal framework had been installed, the judicial process was extremely slow, not only due the lack of judges trained in modern jurisprudence, but also because of the traditional right for all people to appeal, indiscriminately, about any type of case, up to the level of the Imperial Court of Justice, presided by the Emperor himself. This situation created huge delays and havoc in the system, as well as opportunities for abuses by the lower courts. A land case I know of lasted without conclusion from 1942 until the revolution in 1974 settled the matter by nationalizing all land. To cite a personal episode, a lady relative of ours had come to visit from Menz, and we were having lunch with my mother. Addis Ababa radio was blaring about the Emperor's visit to Russia and how a hundred-million-dollar loan was given to Ethiopia. The radio broadcast having terminated, over coffee the lady commented, "Instead of the money, I wish he had brought back one hundred judges" indicating the prevailing dissatisfaction in the interior of the country.

Nonetheless, there was a lot of goodwill and hard work done by the government. There was relatively very little corruption; if any existed it was in the lower ranks. The reason was that the society at that time was small, the economy base narrow, and any sign of wealth outside the normal pattern was easily visible and severely discouraged. The real problem was in the decision-making process: the inherent contradictions that arose between the traditional way of doing things and the dynamic pace required by modern practices. There was ultimately a cultural and psychological barrier between the traditional and contemporary outlooks regarding governance.

CHAPTER 20

The Character and Personality of the Emperor

~

IN REMINISCING ABOUT EMPEROR HAILE Selassie, or any other Emperor of Ethiopia, one must first understand the history of the Ethiopian monarchy, its legends, fables, and myths - notions that are woven into the Ethiopian psyche. According to our history, the Ethiopian Monarchs of the Solomonic dynasty are the descendants of King Solomon and the Queen of Sheba, whose progeny was Menelik I, the first King of Ethiopia. Whether this is real or a myth is not important. Just like Biblical history, it is a matter of faith.

Hence we must reckon that the personalities of Emperor Haile Selassie and his generation were shaped by this absolute faith as framed by the ancient books known as the *Kibre-Negest* or "The Glory of the Kings" written in *Ge'ez* that relates the origins of the Solomonic line of the Emperors of Ethiopia, as well as the *Fetha-Negest* ("Law of the Kings"), a legal code dating back from 13th century. Cultured by religious indoctrination, both through Orthodox classical education and western Catholic influences by his foreign tutors the French Jesuits and having lost his mother at an early age and his father in his teens, growing up in Menelik II's Imperial Court must have been an onerous and challenging burden for the young prince.

The entourage of loyal and wise men to whom his father had entrusted his upbringing was a precious support to mastering and surviving the byzantine politics of the Court. Here we have a man imbued with a fifteenth-century political and social tradition of the State, in a twentieth-century world. A man of exceptional intelligence without formal academic discipline, having visited Europe and met many statesmen and politicians, he must have understood and sensed the importance of bringing Ethiopia into the modern world. Following his predecessor Menelik II, throughout his life, he gave priority to education and to modernizing the state institutions as best he could. During his reign, he succeeded in securing the country's independence and sovereignty; obtaining patriarchal independence for the Ethiopian Orthodox Church; gaining rightful international recognition and respect for Ethiopia; establishing for education for all; returning Eritrea to the motherland and restoring her legitimate seashores; introducing a modern judicial system and codifications of the Laws; modernizing the state apparatus; creating a modern defense force (army, air force and navy); adopting quinquennial socio-economic development plans; introducing autonomy to provincial administrations; establishing banks and financial institutions, airlines, telecommunications, highways, ports, and many other modern structural reforms. This was no easy task when starting from scratch with little money, and scarce human resources. Last but not least, conducting an independent, neutral foreign policy in spite of enormous international pressures of all kinds was no mean achievement.

Obviously, all these changes generated their own dynamics and expectations beyond the capabilities of the State. Moreover, as he aged, the Emperor lost the edge and drive of his early years. Like all one-man rules, he did not build strong political institutions adapted to the present times, as he probably viewed them as challenges to his authority. Neither did his absolute hold on power allow for strong political personalities to emerge. Nevertheless, in the end he conceded graciously to the revolution and did not allow any violent action against the change, although this probably would have been less painful to the country than the cataclysm that followed the fall of his regime. All in all, he left a stable country with an established solid base upon which a modern and prosperous Ethiopia could have been built.

～

The monarch also had his human side; he loved his family and was very loyal to those who served him faithfully, whatever the flaws in their character. He loved animals of all sorts - dogs, horses, lions, leopards, cheetahs were kept in the Palace gardens. As for his attitude towards money and luxuries, from my experience, he was very parsimonious and very simple in his tastes. During his first visit to America, one of his nieces was to join his suite from England. As I was in Paris at that time, he ordered me to buy her some appropriate clothing, which I did with the help of my wife, *Woizero* Martha Nassibou. When I presented him the bill that amounted to about two thousand dollars, he was surprised and asked, "How did you spend so much on clothes?" Another time he was in Berne, on an official visit to Switzerland, and an antique dealer sent him the photograph of a beautiful Louis XIV desk that he was selling. The Emperor liked it and ordered me to go and buy it. I went to the store and saw the desk which was truly magnificent. However, the price he was asking was rather low for such an antique piece, which made me suspicious. I asked the owner if he could provide me with proof that the piece was authentic. He declined and admitted that it was a copy, the original was in Buckingham Palace. When I reported that I did not buy the piece because it was a copy and not the original, the Emperor became very angry, and said, "You did not buy it because you are jealous!". When I explained that he would have been even angrier had I bought a copy, he was silent for a moment then said, "You did well."

I cannot say that I had very close contacts with the Emperor, but I can report that he was generally kind to me, especially during the later years. When I returned to government after ten years, in spite of some people's objections and my active role in opposition politics, he did not deny me my seniority. In fact, I could speak more freely with him than with some of the ministers. He never rejected any proposal I made, provided that he clearly understood what I was suggesting. I believe that he was a great human being despite his human faults, and one of the greatest leaders Ethiopia ever had. He deserves a memorable and honorable epitaph.

As I mentioned earlier, the Emperor in spite of his keen inborn intelligence and vast experience, lacked some the academic background that would have given him a broader knowledge and outlook on modern developments. He knew French and understood some English. I believe that he read some history, but I doubt if he had much time to indulge in extensive reading. From what I observed, his day started around five in the morning and ended around midnight, including a couple of hours for meals and a midday break. He insisted that everything - even the smallest items - be reported to him, by all Ministries and Departments. Any small official, a plethora of which there was no lack of, could - was even expected - to report to him directly. The various functions he attended were strictly scheduled and regulated. He was thoroughly dedicated to his mission and was an indefatigable worker. He regularly attended all Church celebrations, and every afternoon he visited hospitals, schools, and functions where his presence was required. Thus, the Emperor kept well informed of all happenings in the country, which allowed him to keep a tight hold on all political, economic and even social events. For instance, in the diplomatic missions abroad we would receive his answers to our reports regularly by the next pouch, unlike our Ministry, from which we hardly ever received any instructions or information about developments at home or about Ethiopia's foreign policies. In fact, missions abroad were rarely used as instruments of foreign policy.

An incident that I believe deeply affected the Emperor was the death of his favorite son Prince Makonnen the Duke of Harar, in 1957. The Duke of Harar, of whom I had been a close friend, was a very intelligent, kind and generous person. He was friendly and open to everyone. During the years of exile, he attended public school in England. Being young and estranged from the highly cumbersome environment of traditional court life, he had lived in a modern environment from which he acquired contemporary notions of democratic governance that were difficult for the older generation to absorb. He was well informed about conditions in the country because once a week his office was open to the public where he met all sorts of people who had complaints against the administration and tried to help them by reporting their problems to the Emperor. He had a strong empathy for the people, and he always tried to assist those with problems.

~

In the many discussions we had, the Duke was somewhat skeptical about the way the government was running. One could perceive a certain apprehension and wariness in his views, which he expressed with some humor. He died in a car accident about which people gossiped, saying that he was killed by a jealous husband, which was completely false. The day he died he was to have joined the Emperor who was proceeding on a visit Shashamane. I had breakfast with him and Princess Sara, after which he started going to his car to begin the journey when *Ras* Mesfin arrived in a brand new VW Combi. The Duke, who loved new cars, chose to ride with the *Ras*. About forty minutes later, he was dead in a car accident in front of the Air Force base in Bishoftu. There was no way that an assassination could have been carried out. In those days the road surface was gravel, and VW Combis, that were not made for such roads, tended to turn over frequently. Unfortunately what happened to the Duke was that a wooden case loaded in the back was thrown forward when the vehicle capsized, hitting him in the back of the neck. Later I saw his body myself and saw that something heavy had struck him from behind just below his head. I believe that his death was a great loss for the Emperor, and it might have influenced his outlook and attitude concerning both the future of the Crown and his legacy to the country. For me, the death of the Duke of Harar was the loss of a great friend and a protector.

Ultimately, we must judge the Emperor at the human level, with all the virtues and shortcomings that characterize each one of us.

CHAPTER 21

The Government and the Opposition

⌐

As TIME PASSED, THE GOVERNMENT grew bigger, and the country's domestic political and socio-economic requirements for development diversified to a greater degree. As even relatively minor matters had to be referred to the Emperor for his decision; the execution process was extremely slow. Thus governance, especially in later years, became dysfunctional and provided officials with the opportunity to avoid responsibility as well as to engage in all sorts of infighting and intrigues. Nevertheless, in spite of these stumbling blocks, with the infusion of professional talent from returning students into the administration, many structural and basic reforms were initiated. By the same token, the shortage of qualified personnel to manage and administer the new projects at the grass-roots level severely delayed their implementation.

Ethiopia's international relations had also expanded as regards world affairs, the country having become a signatory to many international treaties and agreements. As a result of all these influxes of new ideas and developments, the societal and economic life of the country was changing much faster than the ability of the administration to manage it. A new urban middle class emerged, and it demanded open reforms of the political and economic system and new opportunities. Dissatisfaction with the regime was permeating amongst all classes. Thus some of us decided to organize an underground political opposition party.

As mentioned, I knew *Dejazmach* Takele Wolde-Hawariat from before the Italian invasion. He was the Director-General of the Ministry of Agriculture when my father was the Minister. He was a great patriot, who fought the Italians during the occupation and continued to do so from exile with the liberation forces in Kenya. *Ato* Makonnen Habte-Wold and Takele were first cousins. Strangely enough, while *Ato* Makonnen was a staunch, loyal follower of the Emperor, Takele was persistently against his rule and was in and out of favor of the Imperial Court several times. He had been the first Governor of Addis Ababa soon after the Liberation; his last post in government was Vice Minister of the Interior. He was exiled and placed under house arrest several times due to his political activities, which led to his eventual demise when he chose suicide against detention and humiliation in prison.

Despite the fact he was not on good terms with the Emperor, *Dejazmach* Takele was an unconditional patriot, highly respected by most people, particularly by the former Patriots who felt short-changed and excluded from power by the Exiles group led by *Tsehafi-Taezaz* Wolde-Giorgis Wolde-Yohannes and *Ato* Makonnen Habte-Wold, who were close allies at that time. As the general dissatisfaction with the regime grew amongst the educated elite who wished to play a progressive role in the governance of the country and the recalcitrant establishment, political opposition groups started emerging amongst the civil and military factions. At a social gathering in *Dejazmach* Takele's home, we started discussing the politics of the country and he confided to me that he was forming a political party that had the objective of changing the system of governance - an issue voiced by many. I shared the same views and values because I strongly believed a change was needed to bring the country forward. And I was personally very angry and frustrated because of the shabby and unfair way I had been treated by my superiors, including the Emperor himself, who had believed all the false accusations made against me by the officials at the Ministry of Foreign Affairs. Thus I joined *Dejazmach* Takele's clandestine movement.

The movement did not have a clearly designed political program. The general motto was *"meshashal"* (improvement), meaning change without necessarily detailing what was to be improved and replaced. Most of the members were former Patriots, colleagues of his and some members of the military. From the younger group *Ato* Seyoum Sebhat, a dedicated ideologue, was his assistant. Later, others from the intelligentsia joined the movement. Following countless clandestine meetings with various groups including some military and police officers, we formed the Ethiopian Democratic Party in 1959. The first task was to prepare a political program. Several teams of experts were set up to draft policy papers regarding the various sectors of the country's governance, and we prepared a political program for a democratic system of government. It was about 80 pages long and covered all sectors. *Dejazmach* Takele was Chairman, I was Deputy Chairman, and *Ato* Seyoum was Secretary. While we were organizing the party - a slow process because of the secrecy we had to keep - an event that surprised us occurred, namely the attempted *coup d'état* by Brigadier-General Mengistu Neway, Commander of the Imperial Guard, and his brother Girmame Neway.

~

It was an unexpected *coup*; even *Dejazmach* Takele, who was in touch with many groups and individuals, had no inkling about it. We were distant cousins with Mengistu and Girmame by our connection through our branch of the Moja family. Moreover, we were very close friends. As far as I knew them, both men were very nice people, honest and generous. While Mengistu's character was in the traditional mold, Girmame's had been radicalized by his Western education and leftist influences.

They were both loyal patriots with an absolute dedication to the welfare of the Ethiopian people. Often on weekends, we gathered with family and friends at General Mengistu's residence in the Imperial Guard compound and enjoyed excellent meals. Of course, heated but friendly political discussions took place. This practice ceased after the weddings of the two brothers that took place the same day. After that, we met mostly at the Palace or various social functions. Notwithstanding our close friendship, I personally had no idea that they were planning a *coup d'état*.

It was thus a complete surprise to me when an American neighbor of mine came to my house early in the morning and asked me what was going on because he could not go to his office at the Embassy as armored cars were blocking the road. He told me that he suspected that some military revolt was happening. The Emperor and the Prime Minister were out of the country on an official visit to Brazil and other Latin American countries. I found this a rather strange time to conduct a *coup*. After my neighbor had left, I went directly to my office on Haile Selassie Avenue, near the Mosvold store. On the way I could see a lot of people gathered here and there; something was definitely afoot. From my office, I called General Mengistu's office to no avail. Then I called *Dejazmach* Takele, who confirmed to me that the Imperial Guard had staged a *coup* and that an announcement would be made on the radio around noon. At this point, some friends had come to my office to see what we could do. As I didn't have a radio, we went across the street in front of a shop where a lot of people had assembled to listen to the radio announcement. Military music was blaring for a while; then the Crown Prince read a short declaration about the need for change. The statement was not only short but was also vague as to the precise objectives of the *coup*. And it was not followed by any other explanation, only the martial music that kept on blaring. One thing that I will never forget is a statement made by a member of the public, who said, "This is a matter between the father and the son. It does not concern us. Let's go about our business", upon which the people simply each went their own way.

The first issue on our minds was the safety of our families. Seyoum Sebhat and I went to collect his wife and daughter and then proceeded to my house in Aware. As I had some friends at the British Embassy, I thought that it would be better to take the women and children there for safety. But when we arrived there, the Embassy declined to accept them to avoid any complications that might arise. So we went back to my house and left our families there. Together with Seyoum, and Habte Ab Bairu, who had also joined us, we returned to my office. All sorts of rumors were going around, but nobody knew what was going on exactly, apart from the fact that high officials were being held hostage in the Palace. The day before, Mengistu had lured them to the Palace on the pretext that the Empress was reportedly seriously ill.

The rumor was that the Imperial Guard was going to attack the Army and that the loyalist forces led by Lt.-General Merid Mengesha (then Minister of Defense) and many senior officers of the Army assembled in the Fourth Army Division Cantonment were receiving reinforcements from other Army units. The second day, some sporadic shooting occurred here and there, but no serious clashes took place between the factions. In fact, Lt.-General Issayas and Major Assefa Lemma (Army) made some attempts at conciliation, but to no avail. The Air Force had remained loyal but for a few junior officers. The armored division had joined the loyalists, as well as all the other divisions of the Army. In Eritrea, the Governor, Lt.-General Abye Abebe, and the Army's Third Division had remained loyal. The University students marched to the Fourth Division in support of the revolution but were immediately dispersed. By this time, the Imperial Guard units that had joined the *coup* had started to disband and surrender. In actual fact, the majority of the Imperial Guard, including the high-ranking officers, didn't know much about the *coup*. Apart from the Neway brothers, only a few young officers knew of the plot. By the afternoon of the second day the remaining plotters - Mengistu, Girmame and a handful of their associates - were surrounded in the Palace. When asked to surrender, in a senseless act of desperation they massacred the senior officials they had held as hostages. Whatever their intention, this ignominious act of murdering unarmed elderly people was unpardonable and symptomatic of what would have happened had the *coup* succeeded. It can even be said that it was a precursor of the massacres and villainous murders that occurred subsequently with the revolution of 1974 and today's tribal regime. Killing innocent unarmed civilians and terrorizing the population has become the *modus operandi* of the so-called revolutionary regimes or liberation movements. The sad fact is that those in the West who profess democracy and human rights acquiesce tacitly to this type of violent and corrupt governance, and even sustain it with large amounts of financial, economic aid and technical assistance.

～

On the part of the Ethiopia Democratic Party, we continued our work to increase the membership. The failed coup had opened up a "Pandora's box" for many, particularly amongst the younger officers group, and this enabled us to recruit some them. Unfortunately, some of the leaders were arrested because of various leaks. This discouraged many others, and the government for its part gave many promotions which weakened the movement in the military. One area in which we were nonetheless successful was getting the government to legalize the confederation of labor unions. Many of our members worked actively to organize and give a legal framework for the unions. Ethiopia, which was a member of the International Labor Organization from its inception in 1923, could hardly refuse a legal status to the unions.

At this time, I fell very ill with a bleeding duodenal ulcer that inca-pacitated me regarding all my activities as well as my family life and my business. Ultimately I was treated with surgery in the United States at the New York Hospital. As I had lost much of my physical stamina, my recovery took almost six months.

By 1966, the second Five Year Plan had progressed well, and things were moving in the right direction, albeit at a slow pace. The infu-sion of young and qualified people in the Cabinet gave a lot of hope all around, quelling most of the revolutionary spirit of those advocat-ing radical changes, both amongst civilians and the military. As one of the younger professionals appointed to the Cabinet, *Lij* Endalkachew Makonnen had become Minister of Commerce, Industry, and Tourism. He called on many business owners and asked us for suggestions on how he could help the business community. Some people started by asking for certain measures that would benefit their particular busi-ness. At this point, I intervened and suggested that the Minister should introduce new policies to improve the general conditions of the business environment, which needed serious reforms. My proposal was that the Government should handle licensing, investments incentives, finance and credit facilitations, training on modern business practices and such measures.

The Minister agreed to the idea and suggested that businessmen elect a committee to represent them and submit a detailed proposal for his approval. The businessmen elected *Ato* Tedla Desta, *Ato* Getachew Gabre-Yohannes and myself to represent them. On his part, the Minister insisted that *Ato* Bekele Beshah, General Manager of the Saint George Brewery – a position which the latter carried with arrogance and self-proclaimed importance, be included in the committee. We prepared a draft that the majority of the businessmen agreed to, except for *Ato* Bekele Beshah. When it was presented to the Minister, he responded with a rather surprising answer, asking us to apologize to *Ato* Bekele for unspecified reasons. It became obvious that the Minister had no intention to undertake the challenge of the serious reforms that we suggested. The apology asked from us was completely out of context, and was probably an excuse to please *Ato* Bekele Beshah. In any event, nothing came of the whole exercise.

Business had always been of only secondary interest for me; actually, I was forced into it out of necessity rather than as a vocation. My principal interest was in the political development of the country. Given the promising trend that the country's development had taken, I decided to swallow my pride and return to government service. I considered that changes should be made from the inside, rather than by revolutionary methods which had proven unfeasible and disappointing. I started going to the Palace to perform my *dej-tenat*. I informed Prime Minister Aklilou that I wanted to return to government, and told my mother, *Woizero* Azalech Gobena, who as mentioned earlier was very close to the Emperor and the Head of Women Affairs in the Court, a position she held throughout the Emperor's reign.

CHAPTER 22

Ghana

⁓

My hope was to get a post in Ethiopia, but unfortunately, this did not happen. A few months later I was appointed Ambassador to Ghana. This post was rather secondary, also, as mentioned, our government did not use the diplomatic missions abroad effectively, preferring to communicate directly with the foreign missions in Addis or directly with governments. In fact, the diplomatic corps had become a dumping ground for those who were not desired at home for sundry reasons. I served in Ghana from 1967 to 1970. It was a very pleasant post for me, particularly because of the gentleness and friendliness of the Ghanaian people. I had arrived in Ghana a few months after the downfall of President Nkrumah - a brilliant leader who had placed his country on an international footing and was a prominent advocate of African independence.

Ghana has a long history. The Ghana Empire originally consisted of a much larger area than at present and included parts of Senegal, Niger, Mauritania, and Mali. It broke down into several Kingdoms after the 11th century. It is said that the King of Ashanti at the time could raise an army of half a million men. In due course, the Empire moved south to where the present Ghana is, under the Ashanti Kingdom. In the 16th century Portuguese merchants, followed by the Dutch, Swedish, Danish and British, established commercial relations with the Kingdom, and first the gold- and later the slave trade flourished. By the 19th century, the British dominated the coast and in 1821 declared it a protectorate, which they went on to consolidate as a colony. In the late 19th century, educated Ghanaians started an independence initiative, which forced the British to establish local assemblies, whose role developed into a full-blown independence movement, particularly during the post-World II years.

Dr. Kwame Nkrumah was a major player in all these developments until he became the Prime Minister and subsequently President of Ghana. Unfortunately, he was affected by what seems to infect all African leaders to this day: an unquenchable thirst for power, and an acute megalomania, to the extent that after he had become President, he named himself Osayevo, "The Redeemer," assuming a "deity" status. As the years went by, he became increasingly authoritarian, detaining and persecuting people without any legal course and terrorizing all opposition. The Army and Police supported him until he started organizing a sort of party militia that became a threat to their status. The economy was in a shambles and coupled with an ever-increasing autocratic rule; this led to his popularity falling dramatically. After an assassination attempt, he became more reclusive and started living in an underground shelter in the Accra Military camp. A brilliant man who had done much good for his country and African independence became a victim of his own megalomania. He was overthrown by a military-cum-police *coup d'état* while on a state visit abroad and went into exile in Guinea, where he died in 1972. Elections held in 1969 had brought to power the Busia Administration, but unfortunately, it was also thrown out of office by a military *coup* before it could straighten out the huge economic and social problems of the country. That *coup* was later followed by a revolt of junior Army officers led by Flight Lieutenant Jerry Rawlings, whose regime messed up the country even further for the next few decades.

The Ethiopian mission in Ghana was strictly representative - merely an act of presence - in the African scene with few political, economic or consular functions to perform. At that time Ethiopian Airlines flew twice a week to Accra, the only interaction Ethiopia had with Ghana, except of course the relations through the Organization of African Unity. My activity was limited to sending bimonthly reports about the situation in Ghana and surrounding countries to the Emperor, the Prime Minister and the Foreign Ministry, reports to which only the Emperor ever answered. As before, we were never informed or given instructions about the policies or events that were occurring at home. Our best sources were the newspapers, "*The Ethiopian Herald* "and "*Addis Zemen*", which we received monthly. At the time that I was in post in Ghana, the most important crisis in Africa was the Biafra-Nigeria conflict. The Emperor was a member of the three-member Conciliation Committee established by the OAU which included the President of Ghana at the time, General Ankrah. One day the American Ambassador, the Honorable Frank Williams, a very good friend, called me for an urgent matter. When we met, he said that he had received a message from Addis Ababa asking him to deliver an invitation from the Emperor to the President of Ghana to participate in a meeting of the Conciliation Committee to be held in Niamey in a few days' time. He said seeing as he was the US Ambassador and not Ethiopia's, the task should be mine and not his and handed me the invitation letter to deliver. With some embarrassment, I thanked him for it. When I brought the invitation to General Ankrah, he was upset, saying that he had organized a party for his birthday and that he couldn't make it. Eventually, I convinced him that his presence was very important and that the Emperor, who held him in great esteem, was expecting his participation. I believe that he would not have attended the meeting had it not been for the Emperor's presence.

Otherwise, my mission was almost like a paid vacation, apart from some diplomatic functions and occasional receptions held on national holidays, and attendance at occasional Heads of State visits. Diplomatic life was reasonably comfortable for us, as we could import whatever we needed without any difficulty from Togo or other countries. Lomé, the capital of Togo, bordered with Ghana and had a free port where everything was available, thus it became our main source of supply. As for the Ghanaian people, life was very difficult because of the failed economy. Although some major development projects such as the Acossombo (Volta) Dam, education, social services, communications, infrastructure, and agriculture were given a high impetus during the Nkrumah rule, the internal political instability, and overall mismanagement had hampered the development of a sustainable economy. Having secured their personal positions, the triumvirate of the military, police, and some civilians did not know what to do about country's problems. Eventually, the usual African malaise set in, corruption, nepotism, inefficiency prevailed in the governance of the country. It ended up in another military dictatorship led by erratic junior officers that lasted two decades.

CHAPTER 23

Mission to Sweden as Unrest Grows at Home

~

IN EARLY 1970, I WAS recalled home. When I went to pay my respects to the Emperor, he welcomed me, but he didn't ask many questions since I had kept him informed of the situation in Ghana and surrounding areas regularly. I was hoping to be given some assignment at home, but instead, I was appointed as Ambassador to Sweden and all the Scandinavian countries. A period of about three months elapsed between my return home and my new posting. This wait gave me a chance to observe more closely the developments at home. Moreover, after my appointment, I went around the country familiarizing myself with the various Swedish aid projects, which gave me the opportunity to have a close look at what was happening at the grass-roots level. Swedish aid and technical assistance programs were the most altruistic and successful projects in Ethiopia. Starting with the Genet Military Academy in Holeta prior to the Italian invasion, Swedish assistance continued after the Liberation and was expanded by several new projects. These included: the Imperial Ethiopian Air Force, the Pediatric Clinic, the Building College, the Nutrition Center that developed the famous *"FaFa"* baby food, the Elementary School Expansion program and the Chilalo Agriculture Development Project. The Chilalo project, in particular, had become a showcase for international cooperation in the field of food production. It was a project Robert McNamara visited when he was President of the

World Bank. On the whole, Swedish assistance was a most successful foreign aid program without any political ties.

~

However, other things in the country were not going well. The Emperor traveled all around the world, and much attention was given to African affairs instead of domestic problems. The economy was stable but latent under a lethargic executive body that was entangled in endless intrigues by sundry interest groups wrangling for position in palace politics. Although some good legislation and structural projects were adopted, their implementation was slow and inadequate for the country's developmental needs. For instance, in the early years when trained personnel were in high demand, graduates, professionals, and skilled workers coming out of the University and technical schools were easily absorbed by the civil service and some institutions, mostly in Addis Ababa. As government posts filled, jobs for new graduates became scarcer even in the private sector which was suffering from a lack of incentives and slow development. It added to a general discontent that was prevailing amongst the working class, the students and even in the army and police. Student protests and labor strikes were very frequent in all sectors. However, the government seemed to be unable to take actions to remedy the situation. Everyone was criticizing the government, including the officials themselves.

Together with advancing age and diminishing energy, the Emperor's personal hold on power became ineffective and unworkable. In the meantime, the country had developed substantially on all fronts, and the government apparatus had greatly increased. With the return of many educated people the quality of the administration had improved, and as new projects were introduced, their management became more complex. The demands on public service increased proportionally. Politically and socially diverse interest groups, including foreign influences, were also playing their part. Favoritism, nepotism, and cronyism dominated the political scene. Glaring inadequacy was quite apparent in people holding high positions.

Although all these changes and developments occurred through the initiatives of the leadership, the leadership became a stumbling-block of its own creation. Thus, power was floating between the Emperor whose management system had become inoperable in a bureaucracy to whom he had not formally extended any delegation of power. Ethiopia existed in a leadership equivocality. It is true that quite extensive powers (by Ethiopian standards) were delegated to Prime Minister Aklilou when he was promoted to the full Premiership in 1965. But because of his personality, or maybe because of conditioned reflexes, he never used them effectively. In comparison, at a time when the Emperor had full vigor and energy, and *Ras-Bitwoded* Makonnen Endalkatchew was the formal Prime Minister, *Tsehafi-Taezaz* Wolde-Giorgis, who was only Minister of the Pen (executive secretary of the Emperor) ruled the country with an iron fist by sheer hard work and a dynamic, though sometimes abrasive, personality.

By the late 1960s, discontent amongst various factions of the society had become ever more manifest. Student protests, labor strikes, discontent within the army, the government's lack of appropriate guidance had instilled a general dissatisfaction. When the famine occurred in 1972, despite the fact that there was no lack of resources both in terms of food and equipment, the government was confused and incapable of acting adequately and in time.

～

The new professional class that had emerged on the political scene had turned into a new bourgeoisie interested in its own welfare. Owning a house, a Mercedes car, getting married to a member of a well-to-do family, acquiring wealth and defending one's turf had become the *leitmotif* of the educated elite. Although many of them were highly qualified, their ability to implement new measures was limited by the concentration of power in the Emperor, and also by the back-biting that prevailed amongst them. It was exacerbated by the Emperor's manipulations when he would, for example, make a decision by addressing directly a particular official, which made the others insecure of their position. Sometimes he would call *Tsehafi-Taezaz* Wolde-Giorgis at the Jubilee Palace early in the morning. Informed by his allies, the Prime Minister would also rush there to find out what was going on. We used to laugh when we saw this parody happening. One day I asked General Assefa Demisse, the Emperor's principal ADC and a friend, what was going on. He said they are simply talking about the old days. Nevertheless, I think it kept the Premier on his toes. This method could have worked well in the old days, but in a country that was coming into a modern world with a government that had expanded many times over, it became more of an impediment to any decision-making, and a cause of general inertia and procrastination. It also allowed the influence and interference of people and groups representing conflicting interests. Even the principal valet of the Emperor had some political influence, and the driver of the Emperor's car was promoted Brigadier-General, to the dismay of the officer corps.

The squabble for power between the sundry groups, combined with the lack of effective leadership, had paralyzed the State. The Emperor already in his mid-eighties, after a long and strenuous life, had lost his early dynamism and verve. There was no institution or personality to maintain the continuity of the system with a new creative vigor, as necessitated by the changing growth of the country. The Crown Prince, who was a very kind and friendly person, besides the fact that he was always kept at the margin of the power center, had neither the character nor the inclination needed for strong leadership. The Prime Minister, a well-meaning man, had no political base of his own; his main asset was his close relationship with Emperor, which was jeopardized because the Emperor's decisions were often influenced by other elements in the palace politics. Nor did the Prime Minister have effective control of the bureaucracy; as mentioned, his office consisted of his personal secretary and a couple of staff, with no other mechanism to follow up the affairs of state. Married to a French lady, he had little contact with Ethiopian society and did not seek to build his own support group. This, in turn, deprived him of having a constituency of his own amongst the public, or in the circle of the Imperial court.

As a matter of fact, the civil service at the level of the central government was very good and functioned well; what it lacked were vigorous leadership and a dynamic decision-making process. More than often than not, things were relegated to committees, whose workings were slow and inconclusive. There was in fact very little corruption, apart from some at a very low level.

As mentioned, the Emperor was very preoccupied with foreign affairs, the OAU, and frequently traveled abroad. Traveling abroad to attend any type of conference, whether of important interest for our country or not, had also become fashionable with ministers and young bureaucrats. Life, in general, was leisurely for the ruling class and some business circles. Large-scale farming such as coffee, oilseeds, cotton, sugar, and grains had begun in a few areas but was still very minor compared with the potential of the country. Little incentive was extended to local businesses and entrepreneurs both financially and technically. The investment law was restrictive both for domestic and foreign investors. Thus economic and social development was retarded for lack of government incentive, and by the same token government resources were curtailed by limited revenues. The banking system was a virtual monopoly held by the Commercial Bank and the Development Bank that were both undercapitalized, bureaucratized and incapable of meeting the needs of development. Only one private bank was allowed: Addis Ababa Bank, again with limited capital. Foreign banks were not welcome during the Imperial regime, and even later. For all these reasons, the Third Five Year Plan could not be achieved.

Somehow I felt that the government was floating on the surface while a contagious revolt was brewing underneath. A crisis was clearly evident, even the Ministers and high officials talked openly about it. However, basking in the apparent peace and comfortable lifestyle, nobody was doing anything to remedy the situation. As for Parliament, with subsequent elections, the Chamber of Deputies had acquired maturity with new experienced members, and the Senate was composed of former high officials relegated there as a form of retirement from active duty. In essence both Houses represented a formidable source of seasoned knowledge and a popular forum from which the government could have benefited. But unfortunately, Parliament was viewed by the Court and the administration as an opposition platform. Officials did their best to avoid presenting their cases to the Parliament, and the Prime Minister never went to them to seek approval for the government's policies, although there were some critical issues like land reform that needed broadly based popular awareness and support to overcome the opposition of various influential - but mostly absent - landlords, including the Imperial Court. Personally, I tried to warn the Prime Minister and many highly placed personalities of the looming danger, but my views were seen as extreme and not of imminent concern as they had labeled me as a radical.

~

Thus I went to join my new assignment in Sweden. Shortly after I had presented my credentials to the King, I had my first surprising welcome: Ethiopian students broke into the Embassy and destroyed some furniture. One reason was that my predecessor had refused to renew their passports and had not been of any help to them. He was a good man in our own context, but completely out of his depth as a diplomat. His experience was as head of the prisons department in the Ministry of Interior. As I said earlier, the foreign missions were often a dumping ground for undesirable elements, including myself. He had been appointed as ambassador because of his friendship with the Minister. I ordered all passports renewed for whatever length of time they requested, and remedied the situation. I told the students they were welcome to any assistance they required. The Ethiopian community in Sweden was rather small; apart from the students, there were some political exiles such as Ambassador Teferi Sharew and *Lij* Abate Getachew, who had deserted in support of the Neway brothers' attempted coup in 1960. Amongst the regular residents, there was *Ato* Almaz Tesfaye, a businessman married to a Swedish lady. For me, they were old friends. Except for *Ato* Teferi, who was reticent, I made contact with the others and renewed our relations. Within a few months, I also presented my credentials to Denmark, Norway, and Finland, to which I was also accredited.

Although Ethio-Swedish relations dated from a long time, and their aid program was extensive and very successful, there was an intense anti-Ethiopian campaign in the Swedish press and from some political quarters, particularly about the lack of land reform and democratization. Some frank discussions I held with concerned authorities cleared the air, especially since the Swedish International Development Cooperation Agency (SIDA) officials knew the political problems of the country well. The fact that young Ethiopian professionals were taking over the management of some of the Swedish projects also helped to subdue the opposition; actually, Swedish aid doubled in volume during my tenure. Nevertheless, the Swedish authorities were preoccupied about the future direction of the country, as I was on my part. At the end of 1971, at a dinner given yearly by the Swedish Court for the Diplomatic Corps, the King, who was well briefed about the situation in Ethiopia, called me, and mentioning various projects, he told me, "The Emperor should pay more attention to problems at home instead of using so much of his time traveling abroad."

After this occasion, I took my yearly vacation and went home. As the Emperor was in Asmara, I stopped there to pay my traditional courtesy.

It was also easier to talk to him there than in Addis, without the interruption of one official or the other. I conveyed the message that the King of Sweden had given me and explained some aspects of the criticism we were getting from Swedish politicians and the press. I talked very frankly about how I was worried about the developments in the country. With regard to land reform, the Emperor said that the subject was being studied and was being discussed in Parliament. I said, "Your Majesty, the Crown should set an example by conceding to the peasants the large properties held in its name. This was how the Shah of Iran initiated the land reform in his country and overcame some opposition." I said that the Crown benefitted very little from these properties and that they were merely holding the peasants prey to local officials. Originally, most of the lands were never the property of the Crown; the taxes levied from them were allocated for the upkeep of the Court, while they remained the property of the private owners. It was after the Liberation that they were somehow turned into properties of the Imperial family, without any legal precedent. The Emperor listened calmly, in spite of the harsh comments I made about the government, and said in a somber mood, "We are also dissatisfied about many things. You go to Addis, and we will talk further".

~

At home, things had gone from bad to worse. Labor strikes, student protests and the general paralysis of the government was evident. The famine in the North was ravaging the population of the area. Relatives who came from Wollo to stay with us told us of the gravity of the crisis. Although some officials tried to hide the matter, a documentary broadcast by the BBC spread the news around the world. A new governor was appointed, and a committee formed to handle the issue. While it needed an all-out national effort, the question was treated with the usual insouciance. The old and new elite were busy with their intrigues and political shenanigans; they were all lamenting and criticizing the government as if they were not part of it. I could mention names and particular incidents. However, I find it of little use to do so, and I limit myself to the general apathy of the governing body. In Addis, I was not able to talk to the Emperor, and the Prime Minister had gone to France for his yearly vacation. I spoke with various ministers, informing them of the heavy criticism we were getting from the press in Scandinavia, and the need for some change particularly the implementation of land reform, ideas that I shared. They were all quite familiar with the problems, but were somehow incapable of any practical action, even in matters pertinent to their office. It seemed that everyone was expecting the Emperor to do something. The only sensible response I had was from H.I.H. Princess Tenagne Work, a good friend and a very decent and concerned Lady with whom I could discuss frankly, who told me in very discreet language that, because of his involvement in foreign affairs, the Emperor had some difficulty in following up all domestic matters. Disappointed and very apprehensive of the future, I returned to my post. I talked to the Emperor again in the fall of 1972, when he came to London to receive the Order of Knight of the Garter from the Queen. I reported on the various problems we had in Sweden and insisted again that some serious reforms must be made. Again he listened without questioning, but I could see that he was very tired and unfocused. He told me to discuss the matters with the Foreign Minister, who showed little interest. I realized further how frail the Emperor had become when I saw how strenuous it was for him to board the plane for his return journey.

~

In the early summer of 1973, I was ordered by the Minister of Foreign Affairs to return home urgently, which I did without fully performing the traditional diplomatic farewell. When I arrived home, I went to pay my courtesy to the Emperor, and he was rather surprised to see me. Later I went to see the Prime Minister, who in turn was also surprised. He asked why I had come, and when I told him that I had been recalled by the Ministry, he said that I should not have returned. I was not the only one; other ambassadors had been recalled in the same way. Nobody knew what to do with us. The Foreign Ministry refused to pay our salary, and we were told to complain to the Palace. We went every morning to the Palace to show our presence and to hear the incessant gossip of the many officials hanging around. The daily routine started with the Emperor arriving sharp at nine in the morning; this was followed by an audience with the Prime Minister which lasted about a couple of hours. The Emperor gave audience to other businesses and presided over the Imperial Court of Justice between twelve and one o'clock at which time he retired. In the afternoons, he visited various places and fulfilled some functions between four and six o'clock. I suppose he received some briefings before dinner time. The Prime Minister was in his office for about one hour in the morning and two to three hours in the afternoon. On weekends, both regularly went out of town. Thus, since neither the Emperor's office nor the Prime Minister's had a systematic mechanism to monitor on a regular basis the many aspects of the country's affairs, actions were taken only when particular issues arose. Ministers and heads of department reported when they deemed necessary; otherwise, they simply let matters take their course.

It had become governance by inertia and came across as haphazard. Sometimes I went to the Jubilee Palace in the morning where, apart from the Minister of Defense and the Chief of Staff, all Army and Police Generals lined up every morning to salute the Emperor. This was a new practice that I had never seen before. Some were friends, and I used to tease them by asking when they would start to do their work if they spent half the morning there?

12. *Family portrait - Addis Ababa 1962*

13. *Stockholm, Sweden - On my way to presenting my
ambassadorial credentials to the King of Sweden*

14. *Addis Ababa, 1974, at the Jubilee Palace for my daughter Adey Abeba's engagement to HIH Prince Dawit Makonnen Haile Selassie together with the elders, Lij Yilma Deressa and Dejazmach Kifle Dadi, bridesmaids, and best men*

15. *Geneva, 2013 - With my daughters, L-R Adey Abeba Imru and Saba Imru*

16. Washington DC 2012, interview on Ethiopian current affairs at ESAT television

17. Washington DC, 2016, at the Ethiopian Heritage Society Awards Event

CHAPTER 24

The End of the Monarchy

⁓

IN 1973 BEGAN THE END of the monarchy and the beginning of the most destructive calamity in Ethiopian history, the effects of which persist till the present. The country was in turmoil, and the government was in a shambles. There were all sorts of strikes and protests organized by labor unions, students, bank employees and a lot of complaining was heard from the military. The famine in Wollo was raging, and the government was handling it clumsily. The usual ineffective committees were established instead of treating it as a national emergency that needed the mobilization of all available forces. It was also rumored that the Emperor was not informed of the crisis and that he heard of it first from the BBC broadcast. He went to visit the area, and it was reported that he was appalled by what he saw. More effort was made after his visit, but it was too late to make any difference to the disastrous situation. The students were those who took the matter seriously and tried to help with their meager means. Actually, there was plenty of excess food in the country. With well-organized logistics, the brunt of the famine could have been addressed, and a lot of lives could have been saved. Unfortunately, this tragic odyssey happened when the inexorable decline of the regime had already begun.

⁓

At the end of May 1973, the Heads of State meeting of the OAU took place in Addis Ababa. It was a historic meeting in which the organization, under pressure from Islamic countries, decided to break diplomatic relations with Israel. It was also a tumultuous session for Ethiopia because of Libya's denouncing of Ethiopia as a non-progressive country, and its request to transfer of OAU Headquarters to some other place - to Tripoli, of course. I think that the Algerian delegate had informed our people that the Libyans would be making an embarrassing statement, so the Emperor did not sit in the main assembly hall on that occasion. The response of our delegation was hysterical and almost incoherent until Prime Minister Aklilou took to the podium and gave an eloquent and dignified answer to the Libyan allegations. After the conference, President Senghor of Senegal wanted to visit our historical sites, and I escorted him to Lalibela, Gondar, and Axum. We stayed overnight in Lalibela after visiting several monolithic churches. The President was highly impressed by these extraordinary monuments to Faith. He admired the human ingenuity and physical strength involved in creating such architecture and beautiful art. He talked - rather, lectured me about his view of the world and Africa. He also had a theory that we Africans came from Southern India and that our progenitors were from a race called Dravidians. We returned to Addis after visiting Gondar and Axum.

As I said earlier, the situation in Addis Ababa was very tense, despite the government's pretense of normal activity. I also found myself somehow estranged. I had been out of government for over ten years and absent another six years as Ambassador - a total of sixteen years out of the power center. As I have stated, as ambassadors we never received instructions or even briefings about what was going on at home but for the outdated newspapers we received once in a while. Socially, I was also a bit of an outcast from the new social categories that had emerged during the recent past. First were the would-be upper classes; I did not share much of their pretentious conformity. Second was the newly educated professional class of officials to which I did not belong for lack of a degree, and third were the student groups that I hardly knew. Although I had friends in the various groups, I was more of an observer than anything else. One day I went to see the Prime Minister at his office and asked him to assign me a job or to dismiss me officially, that I was idle and needed to work. He said that he had no government position for me. I asked him to give me a post in his office because he had only one staff and there was no way he could follow up on what was going in the government which had expanded greatly throughout the years. He answered that when needed, he would call the ministers and enquire about their work. Then he said, "Anyway, we are all doomed." (*On est tous condamnés*). I responded that I was not doomed, and left his office angry and frustrated. Then sometime in July, the Prime Minister went to France for his yearly vacation, which astonished everybody because he did not attend the Emperor's birthday celebrations that took place on July 23, at which he was customarily present.

〜

One day in early September I went to the Palace to pay my usual respects when the Emperor called me into his office. There were several ministers and officials present. He said, "We hear that you have become the town playboy." I answered, "Your Majesty, even worse, I have become a vagabond. All work has stopped in the country. What is there to do?" The Emperor was surprised by my answer, but he did not get angry. He simply said, "We will assign you soon," and dismissed me. Some of the ministers followed me out and said that I shouldn't have answered as I did. I told them I had no time to lie and pretend things were alright and that I left this to them. A week later I was appointed as Minister of State in the Ministry of Commerce, Industry and Tourism. The then Minister, whom I had known for years, would not accept me because I was appointed in his absence while he was attending a conference abroad.

Eventually, I was given an office space, but no function. As a matter of fact, I was a superfluous appendage for the Ministry; the colleagues already there were highly qualified professionals who could handle the workload, and even more. Hence, since I was not given any assignment, I decided to find a job for myself. Searching among many projects to be implemented by the Ministry, I found one to establish an Export Promotion and Investment Center (EPIC) that was funded by UNIDO and included the existing Investment Board. As the project had been stalled for some time, the Minister agreed to let me take charge of it. In addition to getting two experts from UNIDO, I recruited some Ethiopian professionals: *Ato* Gabre Admassu, a UK graduate economist as my deputy; *Ato* Ayenew, a US graduate CPA; *Ato* Girma Atnafseged as our Public Relations Officer; and several other young graduates. The existing Secretary of the Investment Board was a trained professional with several years of experience on the subject. We started drafting a revision of the Investment Law and organizing the various functions to promote entrepreneurship and export-oriented businesses.

An important project that I had wanted to introduce as a policy was to allow and facilitate foreign banks and investments to operate in the country. This notion was discouraged, out of fear of foreign dominance of the economy. The economy had not achieved most of the goals of the third and fourth 5-year Development Plans, for lack of financial inputs that could have been obtained from foreign investments. A well designed foreign investment policy would have given a great impulse to the development that desperately needed both capital and technological inputs. Twenty years earlier, when I was Chargé d'Affaires in Paris, I had brought a group of bankers to Addis Abeba where they had proposed not only to open branches but even to deposit gold bullion in the National Bank to guarantee the Ethiopian currency and make it convertible. The proposal had been declined because our financial and banking experts said that sufficient money was available domestically. Two decades later we were facing a serious crisis in the worst conditions, when jobs for graduate and trained personnel, which could have been provided by the private sector, were not available. Although the basic framework and organic laws were already established to allow a rapid take-off, the implementation process was completely inadequate for the pressing needs of the country.

For myself, it was the first time after more than a decade and a half out of government, that I held an office in the central administration. Unfortunately, the situation was not the most propitious to advance any new ideas, for everything was at a standstill. The country was in turmoil; there were strikes all over. Amidst this crisis, the Cabinet decided to raise the price of gasoline, which triggered a strike by taxi drivers and transporters. Parliament raised the issue and called the Minister of Commerce and Industry to explain, which he did clumsily, yet this did not abate the general discontent, even after the price of fuel was reduced. Buses were vandalized, and protests were increasing even within the armed forces. Army units in Negeli-Borena mutinied over bad food and the lack of proper drinking water and arrested their commanding officers including the Chief of Staff who had gone there to find out what the problem was. While all these uprisings were going on, officials (consciously or not) were pretending that things were normal. For example, the Prime Minister gave a big party to inaugurate his new residence. Meanwhile, the revolt amongst the Army had spread amongst all units, including the Air Force, which a pay raise did not quell. Junior and non-commissioned ranks had arrested senior officers, and all order had broken down. Another blunder by the government was to try to justify to the public the introduction of the Education Sector Review, vehemently opposed by the Teachers Association, in an untimely manner in the middle of so much unrest. The teachers all around the country went on strike, followed by nationwide student protests.

With the worsening situation, it was clear that revolution was well on its way. The protesting factions had rejected many conciliatory concessions made by the government. At this point, Prime Minister Aklilou and his Cabinet resigned, and he was replaced by Endalkachew Makonnen, the former Minister of Communications. His appointment was rather bizarre because it had earlier been announced that General Abye Abebe had been appointed as Prime Minister. It was after having accepted the position, when Abye went home for lunch, that he heard on the radio that Endalkachew was appointed in his place. Apparently, some army officers had gone to the Emperor and told him that the Army preferred Endalkachew rather than Abye, and had him change the appointment. I was having lunch with General Abye at that time, and needless to say, we were surprised. When the new cabinet was announced, he accepted the Defense portfolio. I asked him why, and he said he could not refuse because Endalkachew's father was his uncle and he felt that he could help. General Abye was a gentleman's gentleman, a person of high integrity and loyalty to the Emperor and the country. He had been ADC to the Emperor, Minister of Defense, Minister of Interior, Governor of Eritrea and President of the Senate. I think that he knew very well that things were not as they should be. In fact, some years earlier he had written a monograph entitled "Let's correct ourselves" written in a very subdued language, nevertheless criticizing the prevailing governance in the country. A few weeks after he took his post at the Ministry of Defense, I found him in a very depressed mood. When I asked why, he replied, "You don't want to know what this young man (Endalkachew) is leading us into." Having called a meeting with the Armed Forces at the 4th Division headquarters, instead of letting the Minister of Defense who was respected by the Army speak, Endalkachew had stood on a stand and delivered a speech to a tone deaf audience.

~

Meanwhile, all sorts of demands were made by trade unions, students and others. One particular claim was the one by the Congo campaign veterans, who alleged that the government had not paid them the full amount given by the United Nations for their salaries and that they should be paid the sums held back by the government. This was a hot issue that inflamed opinion amongst the military, who supported the veterans since they were asking for pay as well. Moreover, to add to the general confusion, it appeared that *Leul Ras* Asrate Kassa had taken up their case and presented their representatives to the Emperor for a decision and, without consulting the new Prime Minister, had recommended that they should be paid. In any event, the response of the government was that they would check the accounts of the period and verify if the claims were true. However, this did not calm the veterans, who made their demands even louder. Discussing this matter with General Abye, I advised that, given the critical situation, the veterans should be given what they were demanding, which I think amounted to about thirteen million *birr*, because it would bring some calm amongst the military and at the same time would be a good infusion into the market. Unfortunately, nothing came of it.

Endalkachew was well-intentioned, but I think he misunderstood and miscalculated the times and conditions of the country when he assumed the premiership of Ethiopia. He did not understand the political and social dynamics that were propelling the revolution. His noble family background and social milieu, and lack of publicly noticeable performance did not endear him to many factions. When forming his Cabinet, the first people he called upon were *Lij* Michael Imru and *Dejazmach* Zewde Gabre-Selassie, both class contemporaries of his. Both delayed their acceptance, which they eventually gave with visible reluctance. The other members of the Cabinet were young professionals from the bureaucracy who had little loyalty to the Prime Minister; in fact, some were working against him. It took over a month for the

Cabinet to come up with a program for reform, which was rather late, given the rapidly deteriorating situation.

Within months, the committee composed of junior officers and lower ranks from the army and police had consolidated itself as the *"Derg"* (Council). Assisted by some Marxist student groups, it assumed supreme power in the country, with Brigadier-General Teferi Banti as President, Major Mengistu Haile-Mariam as Chairman, and Major Atnafu Abate as Vice-Chairman of the military junta. Other Derg officers were appointed to various ministries, while various civilians considered friendly to the new regime remained in their posts. An inquisition committee against the old regime was set up, which included a collection of professionals such as Bereket Habte-Selassie, a former Attorney General and Mesfin Wolde-Mariam, a Professor of Geography at the University. I still don't understand why, even with a high revolutionary fervor, anyone would get involved in political trials that had no judicial legitimacy yet could involve life and death. I heard that some officials like *Tsehafi-Taezaz* Tefera-Work Kidane-Wold, Minister of the Palace; and Yohannes Kidane-Mariam, Private Secretary of the Emperor, were interrogated very harshly and even tortured. Arrests continued throughout, including the Prime Minister, Endalkachew and most of his cabinet ministers, as well as many officials of the previous regime. Finally, it culminated with the arrest of the Emperor and the Imperial family. Michael Imru was appointed Prime Minister, and some of the former officials started advising the Derg.

～

Our new boss at the Ministry of Commerce was *Ato* Mohamed Abdurahman, a very good friend of mine who had been a member of our group when we formed the Ethiopian Democratic Party with *Dejazmach* Takele in 1959-60. He was issued from a noble Adere family, a great-grandson of the Sultan of Harar, and a law graduate from

McGill University in Montreal, Canada. As was done in each Ministry, the soldier assigned to oversee our Ministry as Derg member was a Mess Sergeant-Major from the 3rd Division in Harar. He and the Minister were quite friendly, as both originated from Harar and communicated in a local dialect. He sometimes barged into the Minister's office with his armed bodyguards and asked the Minister to accompany him to a market where, for instance, it seemed the price of eggs had increased and needed to be stopped. Otherwise, the Minister was most of the time at the Council of Ministers, which appeared to be in meetings continuously, but with few visible results.

Meanwhile, encouraged by the students and some die-hard Communists, the Derg kept arresting people for no reason, or sometimes because they coveted a pretty woman or a nice car. They were confiscating property and looting everywhere. Law and order had completely collapsed. Were it not for the patience and wisdom of the people, things could have been worse. The well-established bureaucracy maintained the viability of the administration in spite of the lack of proper government leadership. On the other hand, the unrelenting propaganda against the monarchy and the previous government by the revolutionary media kept inciting people, with no particular motive other than the destruction of the past. All this was creating a state of anarchy, and the outcome was unpredictable. I knew it was pointless to talk to Cabinet Ministers, for they all seemed to be confused and insecure about their own position. One evening we went with a friend to see the Prime Minister at his house and told him our views about what must be done to stabilize the situation. He listened quietly but did not offer much of his own thoughts.

~

On 16 April 1974, we celebrated the marriage of my eldest daughter Adey with Prince Dawit Makonnen Haile Selassie, Prince Makonnen's son and a graduate of Sandhurst Military Academy in the United Kingdom. According to tradition a senior friend of the family, H.E. *Lij* Yilma Deressa gave away the bride. It was a very subdued affair because of the famine and the general turmoil in the country. Prince Dawit donated the money destined for the festivities to the famine relief. One thing that I discovered as part of the Emperor's true character is when my daughter told me that he said to her while blessing the marriage, "I hope that your father will forgive me for all the wrongs I did to him." Soon after the wedding, Adey and Dawit left for the United States where he was going to a military training course, and Saba, my youngest daughter who had come for the wedding, went back to Europe to resume her studies.

In September 1974, the Derg forced the Emperor to abdicate, which he did voluntarily. Although earlier the Commandant of the Imperial Guard had suggested arresting the military leaders of the coup, the Emperor did not want to cause any bloodshed and surrendered peacefully. Typical of the ignoble character of the so-called revolutionaries, they choose to humiliate the venerable old man further by carrying him out of his Palace in a Volkswagen Beetle, passing through an organized mob vituperating insults at him. Having assumed the supreme leadership of the country, the Derg appointed Brigadier-General Amman Andom as its Chairman. Amman was a very popular officer with the Army, and generally well viewed by the public. He was a professional officer with unquestionable integrity and patriotism. He commanded the 3rd Army Division in Harar and had retired from the Army because of a disagreement with his elder superior, who probably found him too radical. He had been appointed Military Attaché at our embassy in Washington DC, a post he had to give up for health reasons, and he was later appointed to the Senate. When the coup in 1974 took place, he had in reality been out of the Army for more than a decade and had little knowledge of the political developments. Neither did he have a personal penchant for politics. He was a good man put in the wrong place at a wrong time. I used to meet him socially, and on one occasion I asked him why he didn't do something to control the army. He pulled me to a window and pointed out two carloads of soldiers to me. "I can't do anything," he said. "They follow me wherever I go."

For my part, I had decided that there was no way to save the situation and that we were heading towards a highly dangerous state of affairs. I had little choice; because of my relation with the Imperial family, I was going to be arrested sooner or later, a prospect that I found unacceptable. Thus it was time for me to organize my way out of the country. Nothing was happening in our Ministry; in general, the government was at a standstill. The main activity of the regime at the time was to mobilize high school and college students to carry out an education campaign throughout the country, the so-called "Development Through Cooperation Campaign" whereby the students were supposed to teach the peasantry the philosophy and aims of the Revolution. This measure was essentially a very cunning and vicious action taken to disorient and break up the students' spirit morally and physically, especially those from the middle class and urban areas. It was a disastrous and cruel program of mass-displacement inspired by Marxist elements allied to the Derg, and it was implemented by the military. There was little preparation to equip the students for such a venture - no food, no medical services, no lodging, and no transport. Once in place, the students and the ignorant cadre leaders were left to fend for themselves. Girls in their early teens were raped, diseased and abused. Young people were sent to areas different from their own, where they knew nothing about the local customs or even the local language. They had no training or materials for what they were supposed to teach. It was an ignominious plot that caused the death and destruction of thousands of lives. I think that the harsh experience the students underwent eventually marked their mental make-up for a lifetime. I know from my personal experience the traumatic chaos that one goes through when one is up-rooted from one's customary environment and is suddenly faced with the naked realities of survival in alien surroundings.

~

On 23 November 1974, one of the vilest and most cowardly acts in the annals of Ethiopian history occurred with the massacre of sixty-two former officials of the Ethiopian government, including all the senior generals and commanders of the armed forces. These officials had surrendered peacefully; in fact, they were not even arrested. They had responded to a Derg order to present themselves at the 4th Army Division camp, which they did voluntarily. None of them rebelled or tried to escape. The men were taken to Addis Ababa Central Prison, machine-gunned and buried in a mass grave. It was the prelude to the thousands of murders, killings, and assassinations that followed among the factions contending for power, and it ended with the soldiers winning and the virtual elimination of the revolutionaries from the scene. There was an attempt to arrest General Amman who resisted and was killed when he was attacked at his residence with tanks. It was the inglorious demise of the Ethiopian Army and its heroic and noble traditions – a demise from which it has never recovered. Having lost its leaders, and commanded by inferior and incompetent men from the lower ranks, it had lost its morale and sense of honor. Killing one's enemy on the battlefield is a heroic and honorable act, but murdering one's own chiefs and unarmed brothers-in-arms is an act of unforgivable villainy. I cannot describe the state of mind caused by this mass murder. People were horrified and shocked. Several hundred others were imprisoned, and their fate unknown. For myself, many of those killed were close relatives, schoolmates, long-standing friends and colleagues with whom I had worked and lived.

CHAPTER 25

Road to Exile

~

ETHIOPIAN CHRISTMAS FELL ON A Tuesday on January 7, 1975, which made it a long weekend holiday and an opportune time for my escape. I had decided to go to Kenya through the South. The only person who knew my plan was my cousin, Captain Afework Taddesse, who was commanding a police post in Meki, south of Addis Ababa. He was a former officer of the Imperial Guard who transferred to the Police after the failed coup of 1960. He did not agree with the new regime and was afraid of being arrested himself. We had agreed that he would join me anytime I decided to go. I started my journey south on Saturday, January 4. Arriving in Meki, I could not find Afework, so I proceeded to Langano and remained overnight there. On Sunday morning, I returned to Meki, but Afework was still unavailable, so I went back again in the afternoon and finally found him. We drove all the way to Yirgalem and spent the night. On Monday, January 6, we continued south. When we were half way to Yavello, we found that the road was under construction. We tried to follow a maze of dirt tracks used for the construction works where we got lost. Apart from that, I was also afraid of damaging the car, because I had been unable to find a four-wheel drive vehicle, and was using a Peugeot 401 sedan. As it was the Christmas holiday, all the construction workers had left the site, so we couldn't find anyone to ask for directions until we met a peasant who said he knew the direct way to Mega close to the Kenyan border, so we took him along. On the way, we had also picked up an Englishman and his American girlfriend who were traveling from England to South Africa on foot, crossing Ethiopia on their way south. Eventually, we ended up in Yavello, 105 kms away from Mega. What happened was that the peasant, a very smart man, actually just wanted to go to Yavello, so he guided us there instead, getting himself a nice free ride. It was already dark when we arrived, and there was no way we could continue our journey.

At the local hotel, we met an army lieutenant and a police sergeant who were there tasked with escorting 'revolutionary campaign' students on their rural missions. They were tired and haggard. We introduced ourselves, and I showed my identity card from the Ministry of Commerce, telling them that I was inspecting the market conditions along the border. Although they were suspicious of us, they didn't show any hostility. Then a friend of ours, Yohannes Gabregzy, appeared. He told us that he was working for a construction company that was quartered in Mega. He was a younger brother of Tesfaye Gabregzy who had been Minister of Information, one of the high officials murdered a few days before. We traveled together to Mega, arriving early in the morning when the construction crew was breaking Christmas fast. They offered us an excellent breakfast and fueled our car. At this point, I told our foreign friends that we were turning back and that the construction people would find them some other means to continue their journey. I told Yohannes honestly that we intended to continue to Kenya and thanked him for all the help he had given us. He said he wanted to get out of the country himself as they were harassing him because of his brother, that he could be arrested any time and would like to come with us.

~

There were two ways to get to Kenya from Mega. One was a dirt track leading directly to Sololo in Kenya where the border is not guarded but patrolled randomly; the other was the regular route through Moyale, the main border crossing, which we had to take because we didn't have a four-wheel drive vehicle. Once in Moyale, before proceeding to the border post, we went to the local hotel, took a room, and hid a sub-machine gun and a shortwave radio receiver under the bed. It was Ethiopian Christmas day, and the town was very quiet because people had stayed at home for lunch. There was no traffic, and at that hour it was very hot. When we arrived at the border post, there were only two guards, and the gate was simply a small chain across the road. The guards looked worn-out and tired; one of them was actually sleeping in the small wooden shack that was nearby. We gave them some water and asked if we could go to the Kenya side just to look around. One of them responded that yes, it was alright so long as we returned before 5 pm. Moyale village is split between the two countries, and due to the curfew established by both sides, that was the time Ethiopians and Kenyans each returned to their own side of the border. Then something very strange happened. After having chatted with them for a while, when I returned the car I saw that both tires on the right side were flat. Having traveled all the way from Addis Ababa, to find one flat tire a few meters from the border might occur, but two flat tires on the same side, that was very odd indeed. I had my suspicions, but there was nothing I could do. Everything was closed because of the holiday, so there was no way we could repair the tires. I asked the guards if we could walk across to Kenya. Moyale was a few kilometers away, and they agreed again, especially since we were leaving the car in their trust, which in a way was a blessing in disguise.

The village was to the left, and the Kenya administration headquarters were on the right side. When we arrived, I walked directly into the administration compound, introduced myself and asked to see the District Commissioner. Having identified myself with my passport, he received me immediately. I explained that we were asking for asylum as political refugees. The Kenyan officials knew very well what was going on in Ethiopia, and were very sympathetic to our plight. They promised to transmit our case to Nairobi for a decision, and in the meantime, they insisted that we go back to the village because they could not keep us in their compound until they received instructions from Nairobi. Soon enough curfew time arrived, and the Ethiopian officials came across to take us back. I had noticed when we first entered the Kenyan compound that the entrance to the prison was immediately outside the gate. When we reached the main road, I simply walked across and entered the prison with my companions. The guard thought that we were prisoners because we were followed by two undercover policemen and immediately called his chief. The Ethiopians insisted that we should be delivered to them, but he refused and said he must consult the Commissioner first and locked us in a cell. By that time the curfew was on and the Ethiopians retired to their side, threatening to come back in the morning. Our fate was in the hands of God. If we were to be sent back to Ethiopia, our demise was certainly through a very ugly death. Dreading the next day, we stayed awake all night, during which we could hear a lot of noise and movement outside our cell. At dawn, the Kenyan officers came and took us to one of the buildings in the compound and informed us that they had received orders from Nairobi not to surrender us to the Ethiopian authorities. We were to be escorted first to Marsabit and then to Nairobi.

The problem was how to get us out of the compound without creating an incident because the Ethiopians had crossed into Kenya and surrounded the gate. The Kenyans were even afraid that the Ethiopians might come into the camp if they knew in which building we were staying, so they moved us several times from one building to another, and kept saying they were still waiting for orders. Meanwhile, they devised a plan to get us out without warning the Ethiopians officials. Eventually, around 3 pm, they made us jump out of a window in the back of a building, drag ourselves under the barbed wire surrounding the camp, jump onto a big open truck that was parked there, and lie down flat on the truck bed. Thus, pretending to be going on their regular border inspection, the Kenyans arranged for us to pass hidden through the Ethiopian blockade, avoiding any incident that could have provoked a serious confrontation between the two countries. Highest compliments should be given to the Kenyan officials for devising such a successful scheme. A few miles down the road they transferred us into a Land Rover that was waiting there and drove us to Marsabit.

~

Marsabit is a national game reserve about six hundred kilometers north of Nairobi. It is a well-known tourist site with an airport for small planes and a first-class hotel or lodge built on the edge of a large lake and a swamp. Elephants, hippos, buffalo and other wild animals bathe and drink water there. Each room of the lodge had direct access to the lake from where one could observe the wildlife. There was no fence between the lodge and the lake and the animals roamed freely around the area. We were to proceed to Nairobi from there. Unfortunately, however, I had hurt my leg while jumping from the window during our escape from Moyale, and I could not walk. It took about two weeks for my leg to heal. In the meantime, something surprising happened. The District Commissioner and the Chief of Police came to visit me, and after asking about my health they said that there were three Ethiopian men called Mesfin asking to see me, and did I know them? I immediately thought that the Derg people had come in pursuit to take us back or kill us, and answered, "No". They left, then came back a second time and said that the people insisted and were claiming to be close friends of mine. I asked them for a physical description of the people, which they gave me. Their description, coupled with the name 'Mesfin' made me think of *Ras* Mesfin's sons Nega and Daniel, so I asked if they could check to see if one of them had a cut on his forehead and if the second one had a cut on his forearm. Frankly, I don't remember how I recalled these signs; I guess that when stressed our mind works differently. They let them in to see me after verifying the signs I had told them to look for, and as I suspected, they were the Mesfin brothers. However, it was also a surprise for them, because they were expecting to see Michael Imru, who had been Prime Minister for one month after Endalkachew Makonnen. Their father, *Ras* Mesfin Sileshi, had been killed with the sixty-two high officials. Our encounter was most joyful; they had escaped from Ethiopia like we did. They proceeded to Nairobi, while my companions and I remained in Marsabit.

~

My health improved, so we went left for Nairobi a week later. There we went directly to the offices of the UNHCR to ask for some advice and help. The official we saw was arrogant and utterly unresponsive to our request; he told us that they had too many refugees and that we would have to wait our turn to register, which would not be any-time soon. Unfortunately, my companion Afework had no passport and would have to wait to obtain a travel document from UNHCR. As I had a valid passport, I started by looking for a place to go to. Having been Ambassador in Sweden, I went first to the Swedish Embassy but the Chargé there wouldn't even talk to me. Then I went to the British Embassy, where they were very kind and courteous and granted me a visa immediately. Then I considered going to the US, where I knew that there were always opportunities, and where I had some friends. The US Embassy kindly issued me a visa, but the question was, how to get there? I had some money, but I wanted to leave it to my companion Afework if I could get help from somewhere else. I had lost my address book during our escape, and could not contact anyone in the States. In the meantime, the Commissioner of Police in Nairobi called me and said that they could not guarantee my safety, so I should leave as soon as possible. A couple of days later, walking down the street, I met an American friend who used to work at the US Embassy in Accra. I asked him if he could put me in touch with Ambassador Frank Williams, who, as mentioned earlier, had been a good friend while we were both serving in Ghana. He did so, and was extremely kind, inviting me to his house from where we could make the call. After I explained my plight, Frank sent me a ticket to the States.

CHAPTER 26

Work in Development Banking

~

WHEN I ARRIVED IN NEW YORK, Frank and his wife were extremely generous, and kindly invited me to stay in their house until I had settled down. After serving in Ghana, Frank had left government service and become Chairman of the Phelps Foundation. He was also a member of the Board of Directors of Chemical Bank, which was then the sixth-largest Bank in the US. The International Division of the Bank by itself employed three thousand people. Ambassador Williams got me a job at the Bank as a consultant for Africa. Initially, I was working one day a week, for which I was paid one hundred dollars a day. During the following three months, I conducted a risk analysis of about twenty countries in the Middle East and Africa, focusing mainly on their political and economic stability, their leading personalities, and the government structure. The Bank had a large econometrics department with a large databank on each country and many specialists, which facilitated my work.

After I had accomplished this task, the Bank offered me a job as Vice President and Senior Advisor for Africa. Over the next eighteen months, I visited several countries: Egypt, Morocco, Tunisia, Kenya, Zambia, Cameroon, Nigeria, Ivory Coast and Senegal, where the Bank had already established relations. We initiated or shared in syndications for various projects such as LNG (liquefied natural gas) in Algeria,

Cameroon Airlines, and others. Most of the banks operating in Africa were old British and French banks. Looking at the many possibilities that Africa offered, I suggested that Chemical Bank open a branch in Africa, to which the Board agreed.

We opened the office in Abidjan because it offered the best overall facilities and communications, a rapidly growing economy and a well-managed financial structure under the Minister of Finance, Conan Bedie, the driver of the Ivorian rapid development program. When we arrived in Abidjan, Ambassador Léon Amon, a friend with whom I had served in Stockholm gave a reception where Minister Bedie was also present, and the next day we received permits to open our branch – much to the consternation of others, who had waited months for authorization. Chemical Bank had branch offices in the Middle East, but none in Sub-Saharan Africa, where most of the activity was in interbank exchanges and participation in syndications. There was fierce competition amongst the staff, and a gossipy environment that I was surprised to find inside corporate life. The people at the Bank were very courteous and kind to me, particularly my direct superior, Mr. William Turner. Personally, I was well established, I had bought a condominium in Roosevelt Island, and I was financially secure. To be honest, I liked the job, and I managed it well enough. It was well regulated; there was not much room to diverge, but I could use some creative skills in implementation. However, my heart was not in it. My concern, if not my constant nightmare, was about what was happening in Ethiopia.

For my generation that lived through the agony of Ethiopia's destruction and its rebirth, serving our country in its resurrection was an act of faith. I don't know how to describe my state of mind. Ethiopia was the womb from where we were conceived and brought to life; its history was our history, its faiths, its culture, its music, its art and its traditions were the essence of our lives. My family was also there, including all the surviving friends and people I knew. Knowing well the horror and abuse to which Ethiopians were being subjected, there was no way that I could resign myself to my new life and abandon everything that had made me, no matter how enjoyable my present circumstances were.

CHAPTER 27

EDU and the Sudan Operations

~

IN 1975, A GROUP OF Ethiopians in exile had formed the Ethiopian Democratic Union (EDU) in London with Lieutenant-General Iyasu Mengesha as Chairman, H.H. *Leul Ras* Mengesha Seyoum and Major-General Nega Tegegn as Vice-Chairmen. Many other officers and civil personalities had joined them. Concomitantly, we had formed an EDU support group in New York with Bulcha Demeksa, Tessema Makonnen, Desta Girma, and others from the Ethiopian community in the United States. With the strong support of the Nimeiri government in the Sudan, EDU had opened a front in Northwestern Ethiopia and controlled large areas in Tigray, Begemder, Gojjam, Wollo and Afar regions, including the border towns of Abdelrafi, Humera, and Metema. The movement had mobilized a large number of followers amongst the population.

As I was often traveling for my work at Chemical Bank, I tried to pass through London or Paris whenever possible, and thus kept abreast with EDU's operation in the Sudan. Unfortunately, in March 1977 the Derg counter-attacked with a mechanized brigade and re-occupied the Humera area and Metema town. By late 1977, EDU had reorganized and was preparing to regain the lost territories and push towards Gondar city and further into the interior. Bulcha Demeksa and I were invited to attend a general meeting of the EDU to be held in Khartoum, and air tickets were sent to us. It was obvious to me that EDU needed more help because of some contradictory information I was getting from various sources, so I decided to not only go to the meeting but also join EDU in the field. I thus resigned from the Bank, packed my belongings, and went to London where the EDU offices were situated. When I arrived, I was told to wait in London because the meeting in Khartoum would take place at a later date. A week or so later, Asrate Deferess returned from the Sudan and stayed with me in my apartment for several days. He told me that they were broadcasting a radio program from Khartoum that stated rather vaguely that things were alright. I hesitated to rely much on his report and felt it needed corroboration. A few days later General Iyasu also came back from Khartoum but did not come to the office. I could not find him, and he did not return my phone calls. Dereje Deressa returned a week later and informed us again that the meeting was being postponed. At this point, I became very suspicious about the goings-on of the organization, and the strange behavior of both General Iyasu and Dereje. While I was ruminating about what to do, Dereje went back to Khartoum without telling me anything, and Brigadier-General Markorios returned from the Sudan. He told us that the meeting had been held, the party reorganized with Commodore Tassew, a Navy man, as coordinator for all operations, and preparations were made to attack the Derg forces in Metema and push further inland.

I was very disappointed about the behavior and misinformation I had received from the various people and did not understand the reason for such lies. Still, I decided to go and join the forces in the Sudan, for there was no way I could turn back and abandon the cause in which I believed. A few days before my departure, Lt.-General Iyasu and Brigadier-General Markorios came to see me at the EDU office, and in a very vague manner tried to dissuade me from going.

～

When I arrived in Khartoum, the member of the EDU who received me at the Airport took me to a single-story house assigned to them by the Sudanese government. There I met *Leul Ras* Mengesha Seyoum, Major-General Nega Tegegn, Dereje Deressa and other members who were all lodged there. The arrangements were extremely rudimentary; we were each assigned a bed made of rope, and we slept on the terrace at night. A far cry from my two bedroom condo in Roosevelt Island, New York, first class travel, a large expense account, and a dozen assistants! There was no office of any kind – the couple of typewriters that were lying in one of the rooms were full of sand and utterly useless. We met at meal times and discussed nothing but irrelevant generalities. In a private discussion with a member, I learned that General Iyasu, *Leul Ras* Mengesha, and General Nega had gone to Iran to seek help from the Shah. It seems that they had quarreled while they were there, after which General Iyasu had resigned and that is why he had gone back directly to London. General Nega Tegegn had informed the Iranians that he was the leader, thereby creating a protocol crisis and a bitter argument amongst the leadership. Disappointed by this behavior, the Iranians had changed their mind and dismissed the EDU leaders, telling them that they would get some help through the Saudis, who in their turn told them that any aid would be channeled through the Sudanese. It was said that the Sudanese had received three million dollars to this end and that they had refrained from giving it out because of the split and bickering in the EDU leadership. In fact, the Sudan had already supplied the EDU with a large amount of assistance: several thousand rifles, mortars, RPG launchers and millions of rounds of ammunition. It had also provided artillery support at the Battle of Metema, and most importantly, radio facilities *via* Omdurman Radio to broadcast to Ethiopia.

After a couple of days, I asked for a meeting and demanded that we should be assigned some work. The meeting took place with *Leul Ras* Mengesha, General Nega, Dereje as the Party Secretary, and Colonel

Solomon Bekele and his wife *Woizero* Rebka Tafera, a very brave young lady who had also come to the Sudan to assist EDU. When I asked for some details and how we could help, I was told by the Secretary that because it was confidential, they could not inform us of the details of the operation. General Nega said that a complete operational detail was planned all the way to Addis Ababa. In short, we politely were told that there was not much need of us or whatever we could contribute. For me, it was clear that something was wrong, and so I decided to go to Gedaref to see what was happening on the ground. I received a travel permit from the head of the Sudanese Police, Brigadier-General Khalifa, and went by bus to Gedaref at the EDU headquarters. There I met Commodore Tassew, who at that time was going to the front to coordinate the counter-attack against the Derg forces – a confrontation that was to take place in a couple of days. Before he left, he introduced me to *Fitawarari* Kebede Habte-Mariam, Engineer Moges Brook, Major Yosef Gizaw the Operations Officer, and other members of the EDU Central Committee who could brief me on the situation.

The next day, General Nega Tegegn arrived by helicopter with Major-General Souliman of the Sudan Army, who was assigned to handle the support given by the Sudan government. They were to inspect the front on the eve of the attack and make sure that armaments provided by the Sudan government had reached the combatants at the front. *Fitawrari* Kebede and I asked if we could join them to observe for ourselves the events at the front, to which they agreed. The helicopter was a large Russian machine. I think that most of the instruments were not working, apart from the essential ones. It badly needed maintenance, but it looked safe enough to fly. When we arrived at the operations center, there were just a couple of *tukuls* and a grass-covered shade, with no indication of troops - only Commodore Tassew and Colonel Asrat Bogale, a former police officer. When General Souliman asked for the operation plan, Tassew answered that they were to be brought by Yosef, who had not arrived. When he asked if the armaments sent by truck had been received, it turned out that nobody was at the appointed place to take them over, thus they had been sent back. General Nega Tegegn, who was responsible for EDU's defense, was mumbling around pretending to have arranged everything and trying to blame Tassew, who as a Navy man, was out of his depth. I still don't understand why he assumed such responsibility. General Souliman was fuming mad, and we flew to a Sudan frontier post across Metema, where, as previously agreed with the Eritrean Liberation Front (ELF) there was to be a joint operation against the Derg garrison in Metema. In a statement made over Radio Omdurman, *Leul Ras* Mengesha had announced on his own that the EDU supported Eritrean independence, which had caused some controversy amongst members.

⁓

We returned to Gedaref disappointed by the whole mess. I believe that at this point General Souliman, a professional Army officer, with good intentions towards Ethiopia, must have given up on the EDU; because from then on the enthusiasm of the Sudanese authorities clearly faded. As Patriot units were already deployed along the front, the attempt to liberate the Humera area proceeded regardless and ended up with a defeat of the EDU forces. There was also a very serious lack of intelligence. The information received by the EDU was that the Derg garrison consisted of only one company, while it actually turned out to be a fully equipped mechanized brigade. By that time, with an enormous supply of Soviet armaments and the support of Cuban troops, the Derg had repulsed the Somali attack in the Ogaden and was able to deploy a strong defense against the rebellion in the North. Consequently, the offensive to liberate the Humera-Metema area failed, in spite of the valiant sacrifice made by the Patriots against superior forces. The EDU forces had not received the arms, ammunitions, or even the food they had requested. They had to rely on the meager resources that they carried with them.

In a few days, I also realized that the EDU was utterly disorganized. In the border area with Ethiopia, there were thousands of patriot fighters milling around waiting for orders. Many of the leaders like *Bitwoded* Adane, *Dejazmach* Taye Gola, *Dejazmach* Berhane Meskel, Justice Yirga Desta and others leaders from Tigray, Begemeder, Gojjam, Wollo, and Wollega were assembled in Gedaref awaiting instructions. In my estimation, the EDU could have mobilized from one hundred fifty to two hundred thousand patriot forces and many more followers. Ten districts in Begemdir and fourteen in Tigray had joined the EDU, extending its influence in large parts of the north of the country - in Tigray, Gondar, and Awusa regions - and expanded into the interior towards Wollo.

Unfortunately, disagreement amongst the leaders coupled with incompetence in this type of warfare made it impossible to carry out a coordinated and effective struggle against the Derg. A strong resentment had also developed among the rank and file because the principal leaders never appeared in person to visit the front, let alone conduct the battle. As a result, all sorts of factions arose - some tribal, others political.

The problems affecting the EDU were structural as well as strategic. The leadership in the Executive Committee consisted of former officials of the central government in Addis Ababa, with little experience in dealing with the grassroots population or with the kind of guerilla warfare they wanted to conduct. General Iyasu Mengesha, the President, had resigned and the two senior members, *Ras* Mengesha and General Nega Tegegn, were the principal decision-makers. While *Ras* Mengesha was Vice President and responsible for Logistics and Administration, General Nega was Chief of Operations and Defense. As both disagreed on many issues, the command structure was practically paralyzed.

There was no strategy, nor any operational plan, beyond forming a group of patriot fighters to fight a well-organized and mechanized regular army battalion. Neither were there any logistical preparations or supplies to carry out any kind of operation. Funds and equipment gained by the EDU were squandered and already exhausted. Many patriot groups who had joined the EDU and their representatives were in Gedaref waiting for instructions and material help from them. But unfortunately, it was in no condition to provide neither support nor instructions. The tragedy was that hundreds of patriots could not return to their homes because of their association with EDU, which could cause them be persecuted and even killed at home. Many became refugees, and some joined other movements.

Given the total disorganization the party was in, I discussed with *Fitawrari* Kebede Habte-Mariam and Engineer Moges Brook the possibility of reorganizing the movement. Thus we formed a committee composed of various patriot group leaders, and after several meetings, we prepared a proposal to reorganize the party on a realistic and functional basis. The gist of our proposal was to restructure the organization and make it responsive to the real conditions existing in the country and on the front. We suggested that the Executive Council of the EDU should be elected by a general assembly of patriots and that it be expanded to include qualified and experienced group leaders. New strategies and objectives for a new campaign were to be prepared and communicated to all groups, and we needed new command structures with clearly defined functions and responsibilities.

When presented with our proposal, *Ras* Mengesha, as Vice President of the EDU, responded that it would have to be presented to the General Assembly for approval - a meeting that was never called. In any event, as most members of the General Assembly were already in Gedaref, we had already consulted them, and some of them having participated in the preparation of our proposal, we were assured of their support.

Thus we decided to proceed with the implementation of the new program. A new executive committee was elected, and the various patriot leaders present in Gedaref were asked to join their individual units in the interior. Nevertheless, many felt that a confirmation by the EDU leaders recognized by the Sudanese Government was necessary. General Nega, who was in Gedaref, knew of the new set-up and had approved it rather half-heartedly. As *Ras* Mengesha was in Khartoum, I went there to inform him of the new structure that had been adopted. He was not happy. He felt that we did not give due recognition to all the work they had done previously to organize the EDU, which was not the case. However, conditions had changed, and new measures had to be taken to accomplish the goal of the organization, which was in danger of disintegration. Nonetheless, we held many meetings with all members and the leadership, but to no avail.

In the meantime, for lack of direction and resources, the EDU started to break up into tribal factions: Tigre, Amhara, Oromo, and sundry local political groups. Realizing that the movement had become dysfunctional and incapable of countering the regime in Ethiopia, the Sudanese government reduced its assistance.

In view of these events, I decided to return to the US towards the end of 1976, in the hope that we might get some help due to the increasing Russian and Cuban presence in Ethiopia, which risked being extended to the rest of Africa. Having prepared a memorandum to this effect, I submitted it to Mr. Paul Henze who was the responsible official for Africa at the White House during the Carter Administration. He informed me that the US had decided to normalize its relations with the Derg regime, and would not be interested in supporting any opposition parties. Although the US sponsored anti-Derg radio broadcast from

Khartoum continued, it renewed its relations with Ethiopia. In fact, the US later played a major role in getting Mengistu Haile-Mariam out of the country to Zimbabwe and arranging for the TPLF/EPRDF (Tigray People's Liberation Front/Ethiopian People's Revolutionary Democratic Front) to take over power in Ethiopia.

In closing this period, I would like to pay homage and my highest respect to the thousands of patriots and leaders ranging from farmers, traders, military and civilians of all classes that had joined the EDU, for the enormous sacrifice they made with their heroic struggle. The mental and physical agony that we all underwent during these times is inestimable.

CHAPTER 28

Return to the US and the AAPO

~

IN THE FOLLOWING YEARS UP until 1991, my activities in Ethiopian politics were from the periphery; I did not join any particular party. I followed events closely and occasionally wrote papers about occurring developments. In the Sudan there were some thirty opposition groups against the Derg, mostly competing against each other. Eventually, the TPLF that was assisted by the EPLF (Eritrean People's Liberation Front) and was better organized with clearly defined objectives dominated the other groups. It was able to form the Ethiopian People's Revolutionary Democratic Front (EPRDF), a coalition that included the Oromo Liberation Front (OLF), the Oromo People Democratic Organization (OPDO), the Ogaden National Liberation Front (ONLF) and some other minor parties. The TPLF/EPRDF group, claiming to have abandoned its Marxist ideological stance, at least officially, became the favored faction of the United States from whom it received political and material support that enabled it to take over the government in Ethiopia.

I restarted my consulting services and joined the Technical Transfer Institute at the American University in Washington DC for a project to be implemented in Haiti. Unfortunately, a colleague and I arrived in the country after a change of government had occurred and the situation was highly unstable. Our Haitian counterpart was a gentleman called Monsieur Jolicoeur, a very civilized and knowledgeable person, who introduced us to the appropriate officials, who in turn could not initiate the project because of the prevailing political crisis. The country looked desolate; tourism had ceased completely, and everything was at a standstill. My colleague and I stayed in a nice hotel in downtown Port-au-Prince, where we were the sole customers. We had to abandon the project for lack of any response from the government.

⁓

Back in Washington DC, I encountered an old friend from Ethiopia, Katherine Chang Dress. She had grown up in Ethiopia because her father Dr. Chang, who worked for WHO, had established the Medical College in Gondar. She had graduated from Haile Selassie University and later from Vassar in the US. She introduced me to James Gee with whom she had a business venture. Together, we formed a company called Overseas Business Associates (OBA) that offered consulting services to government and private entities concerned with investments worldwide. Our first mission was to China on the invitation of Katherine Chang's connections there. So in 1983, we traveled to China via Hong Kong to Guangzhou. Accompanied by some officials and business managers, we visited by road all the areas bordering Hong Kong, including Macao, which were the manufacturing base for all Hong Kong exports - garments, electronics, watches, jewelry and scores of other goods. From Guangzhou, we proceeded by train to Beijing, a long journey that took over a day. The train journey was comfortable and the service very good.

In Beijing, we were introduced to some high officials to whom we presented our objectives to explore investment and business development possibilities between American and Chinese companies. The officials welcomed us warmly and received our initiative enthusiastically, making all necessary arrangements to facilitate our meetings and visits with business and industrial concerns. They were particularly courteous to me when they learned that I was originally from Ethiopia. They recalled Emperor Haile Selassie and his opening relations with China with praise, stating that these were two countries that shared common traits as historical nations. After visiting many industries and holding meetings with managers and businessmen, we also had the chance to visit the famous Great Wall of China and other historical sites and museums. Otherwise, this being the aftermath of the Cultural Revolution period, most things were in shambles and the general atmosphere still depressing, even food was not easily available for the average population.

We also met with some known artists and writers who had survived the re-education camps, some of whom had suffered physical injuries. Having established preliminary contacts with businesses around Beijing, we returned for the second time in 1984. On this occasion, our activities were centered in Shanghai, which was the principal business and financial center. There were no US Banks operating in China. But for Citibank that had an office in Shanghai, others foreign banks operated out of Hong Kong. After establishing working relations with many business concerns in Shanghai, we visited Anhwei province which has one of the largest reserves of coal in the world. Wherever we visited, the demand for new equipment and capital was general and urgent. At the end of our visits, we had obtained the mandate of some thirty companies, ranging from breweries to steel plants to look for investments and partnerships from the United States. Although the Chinese projects had a high profitability potential, the US business concerns that we tried to interest were not responsive. Doing business with China was viewed with skepticism in the United States at that time. Eventually, we had to give up the China project for lack of sufficient resources. It is only after five years, in 1989, that investments in China became popular.

Comparing what China has achieved today with the conditions in the early eighties, what they have achieved in the short span of thirty years is simply miraculous.

~

While I worked on my business activities, I continued to follow developments in my country. In fact, I traveled to Ethiopia as soon as the fall of Derg regime was announced in 1991. I witnessed the installation of the EPRDF Transitional Government, the creation of a federation of states organized along ethnic lines, and the official separation of Eritrea from the motherland. While this was going on, the OLF (Oromo Liberation Front) (that had meantime withdrawn from the Transitional Government) were murdering, torturing, raping and enslaving Amharas in Arbagugu, Bedeno, Harar, Arsi and other Oromo areas. Thousands of men, women, children were killed, villages burnt, churches indiscriminately destroyed and people displaced from places where they had lived for generations. These atrocities caused a tremendous uproar on the part of the Amhara population and resulted in the creation of the All-Amhara People's Organization (AAPO) under the chairmanship of Professor Dr. Asrat Woldeyes. Professor Asrat had been Emperor Haile Selassie's private physician and was professor of medicine at Addis Ababa University. During the conference to establish the Transitional Government, Professor Asrat Woldeyes had represented the University Union and had voted against the separation of Eritrea, which did not endear him with the TPLF. As to the AAPO, it was not set up as a political party, but as a protest body against the massacre of the Amharas. Later the organization claimed that it was forced by the regime to become a political party, an action it should have taken on its own initiative from the start, as that it might have given AAPO a legitimate seat in the Transitional Assembly, even as a voiceless minority. I did not join them at the time because of the equivocal position they had taken in the political development that was taking place. I stayed in Addis for about two years. I had started starting writing about the general situation in a bi-weekly publication owned by a friend entitled "*Iyeeta*" ('Outlook' in Amharic). Unsurprisingly the paper was shut down by the government in a few months. Observing that the governance was developing towards a totalitarian system, I returned to America.

There I joined the AAPO support group that was also the largest political opposition in the Diaspora. In 1994, Professor Asrat was arrested, accused of sedition against the regime and condemned to a two-year prison term during which he fell ill and later died for lack of proper medical treatment. While he was sick, the leadership of the party had fallen to some minor party officials who almost destroyed it until a new group under the leadership of Engineer *Ato* Hailu Shawul took over. The new group had revitalized the membership with younger active elements and campaigned all around the country. They succeeded to register AAPO in 243 *woredas* (districts) out of a total of 520 *woredas* in all 15 provincial zones of the country. In July 2003, the party held a national convention in Addis Ababa, to which the US support group was invited. I participated in the convention as a delegate of the support group. About three hundred fifty people including guests were present at the convention. The majority of the delegates came from farming and village communities. Amongst them were some teachers, small merchants, and trade unionists. Over half were funded by their communities, which must have entailed a heavy sacrifice for impoverished people who barely manage to keep alive. What was greatly admirable was that they came from all corners of Ethiopia at great personal risks of persecution, imprisonment, beating, dislocation and even death at the hand of the regime's cadre and *Kilil* (Region) officials. Given the vast diversity of the localities represented by the participating delegates, the gathering was truly Pan-Ethiopian, in which an unmitigated and genuine grassroots "popular voice" was heard in diverse languages - Amharic, Tigrigna and Oromiffa and Somali. What was most impressive was the seriousness and sobriety with which the dialogue was carried out throughout the Convention, considering the debilitating life conditions of the people. I spoke and discussed with many delegates. I must confess that I was highly impressed by their profound knowledge and understanding of the country's problems. Their perceptions and aspirations were based on the realities of daily life in Ethiopia, unfettered by the imaginary assumptions that the learned class elite tends to believe as true. The convention was concluded successfully changing the name of the organization to All Ethiopia Unity Party (AEUP). Subsequently, national elections were held in 2005 in which the AEUP participated jointly in the *Kinijit* or CUD *(*Coalition for Unity and Democracy) that ended up sadly with its disintegration and the profound disappointment of the very large public support it had gained.

CONCLUSION

~

THE FOLLOWING ARE BROAD BRUSH-STROKES of my personal outlooks about the epoch in which I have lived and strived. I leave the descriptive details of events and facts to professional historians. The 1974 revolution that replaced the Imperial Regime gave birth to an era of terror and lawlessness. Since then, Ethiopia's historical past has been subject to many interpretations according to the ideological, political and personal persuasion of the narrator. Although a lot of well-researched books and papers have been published by Ethiopian and foreign authors alike, there also a lot of writings that borders on the surreal, particularly those by political bodies and their members. Assumptions, speculations, misquotations, fabrications and exaggerations make poor history.

In my view, Ethiopian history has changed by somersaults during the past nine decades, especially after the Italian invasion of 1936. The post-Menelik period was a time of internal contentions. The *Lij* Iyasu regency concluded with the crowning of Empress Zewditu Menelik and the crown passing to Emperor Haile Selassie upon her death. Thus began the embryonic modernization of Ethiopia's polity with Haile Selassie pursuing Menelik's policies, introducing a Western-style education system and other modern reforms. A written Constitution was adopted, and Ethiopia became a fully-fledged member of the League of Nations. The 1930 Constitution marked the beginning of a constitutional form of government and the end of feudalism which was further diminished by the Italian occupiers who introduced a colonial administration system. Although the occupation only lasted a turbulent five years, it radically changed all aspects of the Ethiopian way of life. Primarily to consolidate their occupation and secure the future development of what they perceived to be their colony, the Italians built a network of roads and infrastructure throughout the country. This factor revolutionized the traditional political, social and economic structure of the nation, by facilitating large population movements and commercial exchanges amongst the various provinces. A uniform system of governance was also introduced and a bureaucracy established that radically transformed the feudal relationship between the rulers and the people.

～

The post-liberation era 1941-1973 was a time of re-establishing the State and maintaining the integrity of the nation. Thanks to the popularity of the Emperor and the patriot forces, the country remained united. The challenge was extremely onerous, beginning with the task of establishing a new government administration. There was no money, apart from a small loan granted by the British; there was no trained personnel apart from a handful of people with formal education; and there was no equipment of any kind as the British forces had taken away anything movable - even office and household furniture. All the Italians were also evacuated, depriving us of technical labor. In spite of the difficulties created by the British in the early years, by 1960 the government was firmly established. Organic laws were codified, and the National Bank and a national currency, the Commercial Bank, Ethiopian Airlines, the Highway Authority, the Telecommunications Board and many other institutions were established and structural changes made. Eritrea was united with the motherland, enabling Ethiopia to regain direct access to the sea.

However, the political system did not evolve in step with the innovations the country underwent with its socio-economic development and its exposure to the world. Addis Ababa had become the headquarters of the Organization of African Unity (OAU); the United Nations Economic Commission for Africa (ECA) and enjoyed the presence of many International organizations, thus increasing the country's role in world affairs. Nevertheless, domestically all power remained centered in the Emperor, all officials were by appointment. Furthermore, Parliament, although partially elected, was in fact only an advisory body with limited prerogatives. Lulled by his worldwide popularity, the Emperor became more focused on world affairs than those of the interior. The first shock came in 1960 with the Mengistu Newaye attempted *coup d'état*, which culminated in the senseless murder of some of the most important leaders whose voice influenced all imperial decisions. Unfortunately, neither the Emperor nor his government learned much from this tragic event. Although the country was fermenting with discontent in all classes of society, things went on as usual. Triggered by the famine in Wollo, this period climaxed with the 1974 revolution spearheaded by students and joined by the military. To their credit, the Emperor and all high officials surrendered all powers peacefully to the revolutionary, although their peaceful surrender did not prevent their eventual assassination.

Thus began Ethiopia's tragic odyssey. The revolution started with a lot of good intentions and a total ignorance of the country's conditions, or about what should be done for the future. The student movements that spearheaded the revolution were enthused by various notions of Marxism, Cuba and the Leftist revolts of the 1960s in the West. Slogans such as "Land to the Tiller" had some popular appeal (although land ownership in Shewa, Wollo, Begemdir, Tigray, and Gojjam was already communal). They claimed it was a matter of returning the ownership to the "tiller" who was already in place in his ancestral land. The actual intention was to disown the people of any property, and take full

control of the peasantry that constituted almost 90% of the population. The same goes for the campaign of "*Idget Behibret*" (Development
through Cooperation), whereby high school teenagers were dispersed
around the country to supposedly foster a kind of development nobody
knew anything about, including its authors. Again, this was contrived
to break-up the student movement from growing into a political force
on its own. It was also a maleficent program designed to decimate the
middle class. Thus a whole generation of youngsters was thrown into
an unplanned and disorganized foray, where many were raped, became
diseased, maimed and perished.

$$\sim\!\!\sim$$

The revolution turned into a murderous struggle for power amongst the
revolutionaries themselves, one faction allying itself with the ignorant
and uncouth military subalterns and providing them with some half-
baked Marxist political ideology. Eventually, the military took over all
the power, after a campaign of terror and mayhem in which thousands
of innocent young people lost their lives. Millions lost their livelihood,
their property and every modicum of basic rights. The governance of
the country fell to a regime with no moral compulsion of any kind
but brute force and unbound lawlessness. After seventeen years of mis-
rule that destroyed and tainted the historical and traditional values of
Ethiopia, maligned its institutions and cultural vestiges and denigrated
its defense establishment, the country was left totally bankrupt to the
vagaries of an unpredictable future.

The power vacuum left by the Derg regime has been replaced by an
ethnic cabal in the guise of an alliance of sundry liberation movements
led by the TPLF. Admittedly, they fought the Derg and won the battle
on the ground, but they also abandoned their Marxist leanings for the
semblance of a democratic platform that won them the support of the

US and other powers and world institutions without giving up their ruthless and corrupt governance. They have conceded independence to Eritrea, thus landlocking Ethiopia, as well as transferred a large amount of national territory to the Sudan. Ownership of the land having passed to the State - thereby to whichever party is in power - millions of acres of prime land have been sold to foreign investors on concessionary terms. Under the governing tribal oligarchy, all economic and financial institutions are owned and controlled by the regime through state- or party-owned corporations and affiliates. Large infrastructure projects such as dams, railroad, highways, industrial and agricultural projects have been undertaken through international, bilateral loans and private investments. Depending on the source, the Ethiopian economic development has risen from six to ten percent a year in the last decade, resulting in a huge disparity of income which has left 98% of the people in wretched poverty, and endowed Ethiopia with the highest brain-drain in the world. Debt servicing has also risen over $1.2 billion per year, in addition to capital evasion that amounts to more than $20 billion since 2004. Corruption and malfeasance at all levels of governance are the *modus operandi* of the regime, with the extensive political and financial support of the US, the EU and sundry "democratic" countries.

Presently, we have entered a new year, 2008 (Ethiopian Calendar), and new national elections have been held with concocted results of 100%, like the preceding one when the TPLF/EPRDF won by 99.6%. The emergence of a burgeoning middle class seeking to maintain its status in a stable and lawful political system, plus foreign elements wanting security for their investments, may induce the regime to give some political space to selected parties. Nevertheless, in spite of all the political gerrymandering, sooner or later the failure of this deficient regime is inevitable.

The question is: What bodes for our country after the present tribal clique loses power in one way or another? Is it going to be a tribal battleground for parties contending for power of some kind? Or even secession? Or - a most likely outcome - another civil-cum-military dictatorship replacing the present oligarchy? Where are the Ethiopian people in all this tumult being played over their destiny? What do the powerless multitudes of opposition factions promise? Will it be another half-baked compromise under the macabre dance of peaceful struggle, or political reconciliations over the head of the real stakeholders, the people of Ethiopia?

The following is a personal comment for those indulging in the politics of our country; it should not be construed as a self-promotion. Given my age, I am quite conscious of my individual limitations. I merely want to impart my views about the future politics of our country. This message is mainly addressed to the young generation, although it does not exclude the veterans of our political mêlée, apart from those with an unsavory past as high officials of the delinquent Derg regime. After all, politics are implemented by people, and their successes or failures are measured by their integrity and irreproachable behavior.

When in 1948 we joined the UN forces in the Korean conflict, the standard of living of the Korean people at that time was no better than our own, and the same could be said of China's after the traumatic ordeal of the Cultural Revolution. When I visited Panama in 1949, but for the American base and some official sites, the city was a slum with a couple of hotels and sundry shops. Today Panama rates 61% on an international scale of well-being. While these countries and others around the world have achieved a high degree of development, why have we failed? Is it not a legitimate question to ask ourselves?

Ethiopia is a great country with a history dating back from ancient times. Our land is varied and rich, containing substantial natural resources of all kinds, from agriculture to minerals, as well as abundant water and energy potential. The Ethiopian people are intelligent, courageous, cultured and diligent in all endeavors. Their social mores and moral values are second to none. With all this spiritual and material wealth in our hands, shouldn't we have achieved higher standards of living for our people? Why have we become a swarm of terrorized and servile citizens deprived of their birthright in their own country? Ethnic and cultural divisions have been imposed on us by the point of the gun, creating disharmony and animosity amongst people. It is time to say NO to this unjust and abusive rule.

The remedy for this sad situation is a national democratic political movement genuinely geared towards restoring freedom and justice to the people of Ethiopia. It is not ideas and methods that are lacking. A plethora of political programs have been put forward by many parties; most of them are advocating for democratic principles on their own terms. However, the personal rivalry and diverging objectives that prevail among leaders have impeded the formation of a united national front. Consequently, no party has been able to establish a constituency large enough to play a leading political role. The only successful political coalition was *Kinijit* (CUD*)* whose winning of a popular majority was forcibly revoked by the regime in 2005. *Kinijit's* ambivalent leadership was also instrumental in its demise.

Assuming that the regime will remain in power for the next five years, I believe that the opposition must belong to the young generation whose future is at stake. They would have the contemporary vision and the energy to regenerate and build a new Ethiopia. In fact, this is already occurring in the country where the youth have taken the vanguard of the democratic movement as exemplified by Skender Nega, Andulam Arage, Reeyot Alemu, the "Group9" bloggers, scores of journalists and activists, as well as the Semayawi Party and countless others who are persecuted and imprisoned around the country. What they need is strong support from all elements of the society, particularly from the community in the Diaspora that enjoys freedom of action with abundant human and material resources.

Unfortunately, the opposition parties in the Diaspora are fragmented and the leadership still tied to defunct notions and groups that do not reflect the present realities in Ethiopia. Neither have they been a voice convincing enough to influence the foreign affairs establishments of relevant countries. Win or lose, the struggle for freedom is at home; aspiring for power over ninety million people from ten thousand miles away borders on the fantastic. Internally Ethiopia does not lack talented people capable of leadership. I believe that the youth in the Diaspora should organize itself into an effective and credible pro-democratic movement representing and supporting legitimate democratic parties at home, instead of wasting time in useless pal-talk and sundry debates. An undeniable fact is that the political movements and regimes that followed the monarchy have failed Ethiopia. That is the saga of this sad era in which two generations of young Ethiopian lost their lives, and a promising future is still to be written. It is time to open a new page of Ethiopian history.

Forty years have passed since the revolution occurred, two generations have survived, a third is on its way to maturity, and the population has increased two-fold. In these four decades, the Ethiopian people endured the abusive and corrupt rule of a military gang for seventeen years, and now for the past two and half decades the no less coercive and unscrupulous governance of TPLF, the ethnic cabal, and its tribal acolytes. Notwithstanding, albeit motivated by self-interest and greed, and with heavy support by the United States, the World Bank, IMF, Britain, other Western powers and especially China, a substantial economic and social transformation has occurred under the new regime. Nevertheless, the polarized ethnic fiefdoms upon which the present political structure is built have been no panacea for the grave problems that the people face in daily life but for the few in power and their collaborators. All the ills of underdevelopment still afflict the vast majority of the population in spite of the billions of dollars in foreign aid and investments that have been poured into the country.

~

THE RECONSTRUCTION OF ETHIOPIA
By Ambassador Imru Zelleke
April 23, 2017

A letter to the people of tomorrow

You are in your twenties and thirties, you have grown up in one of the most painful eras of Ethiopian history, you have been traumatized by the violence and misery that you have endured and seen since your birth. All you have learned and viewed from your unhappy experience is the ever increasing poverty and the wretched existence of your people, including your family and kin. All this spiritual and physical flagellation has certainly left you with some bitter view of your country, especially that it is a homegrown calamity that started with good intentions and ended in a catastrophic cataclysm.

You identify yourselves mostly as Ethiopians, for better or worse, because it is the only origin, history and culture you can identify with, and for its worldwide recognition. You also enjoy Ethiopian cuisine, music, humor, manner and style, and that your civilization is second to none in the world. You can quote your history from ancient times, and you are a repository of two great religions, Christianity and Islam. All this heritage and the gifted talents of our people should have given you a springboard to create a modern and dynamic nation. But instead of building our future on the basis of our wealth and traditions, we fell victim of ideologies and notions that had already failed their own authors.

It is true that our inherited monarchical system of government had, even by its own reckoning, seen its days. Nevertheless, based on its traditional responsibility to rule the nation the best it knows how, it had introduced many positive reforms that constituted a good foundation for the future. Yes, it was not democratic, yes it was oppressive, but compared to what followed it might be called almost liberal. Thus, began a deconstruction and unbridled mystification of Ethiopian history and the invention of the evil "bully" the "Amara" oppressor. According to the new myth, the Amaras, who inhabit the regions of Gondar, Gojjam, Wollo and Shewa have a higher standard of living than Americans, which they gained by exploiting the rest of the population. If you visit those areas you won't see their wealth because they make it invisible by some mysterious magic.

Thus, coming out into the light from the dark cloud of mystifications, it would be pertinent to ask of what and of whom this Amara polity is made. As you all know, a political group holding power cannot exist without allies and fellow travelers with a vested interest in the system. Even presently the TPLF has its own Amara, Oromo, and other allies. There has been a continuous population movement in the whole area, resulting in a miscegenation of races, ethnic groups and tribes throughout the centuries; our rulers spring forth from the same historical process. No Ethiopian can claim racial purity and unique ethnic identity; all of us are of mixed origin, but for some cultural trends that differ amongst the many entities that make up the nation. As to political power, the dominating group of the last one and a half centuries has been a mixed hegemony, from the monarchy down to the lower ranks. Therefore, the claim that there was an oppressive regime composed solely of an Amara ethnic group is utter nonsense. If the Amaric language was preponderant and become the lingua franca of the nation, it is because of its age-old alphabet and written religious and literary traditions, as opposed to the prevailing oral vernaculars. The monarchs Menelik, Zewditu, Iyasu, Haile Selassie, Negus Mikael, and all the great leaders Gobena, Habte Giorgis, Balcha, etc., were of mixed ethnic origin. Hence, if there were oppression and malfeasance by one ruling regime or another, the guilt must be shared by all and not attributed to some fictitious character created to justify a political agenda. It is perfectly legitimate for one to espouse a particular social group and culture, but to use it as an instrument for the deconstruction of a nation that has been built by the blood and guts of millions of people from many origins is unacceptable, and not conducive to a healthy and prosperous future.

This year when Americans are celebrating the 253rd year of their independence, we Ethiopians should be proud to celebrate our thousands of years of independence, despite the many crises caused by our faulty governance. Unfortunately, we lament past misdeeds and negate our own role in the making of our disastrous fate, without devising solutions for our predicament. We are told to forget the past as if it were not the foundation of our existence. We are advised to look to some indiscernible future where milk and honey will be plentiful, and our whims and wants will be fully met. Which divine power will bestow upon us all these blessings? It is a good question to ask. In 1974, we were told to forget the past and look towards a prosperous future in a free and just society, but we all know what happened after that. In 1991, we were promised the same, and we all know the results. Now we are promised the same again and are asked to consent *a priori* to the eventual ethnic breakup of the country, and accept a promissory note from political parties of doubtful consistency and popularity. Is this a promising future for a country that is barely able to get out from abysmal poverty? Is this what the Ethiopian people aspire to for their salvation?

We must build our new Ethiopia on solid bases, on our common history and common heritage. We are not a people sown on this Earth like wild weed. We are civilized people of the first order, our tradition, cultures and values are universal. Our people are talented and our land fertile and rich. Let's make the Ethiopian renaissance with a national spirit and rejuvenating outlook, instead of indulging in endless willy-nilly political deals that promise an uncertain future. In 2005 when more than two million people demonstrated openly in Addis Ababa and later when twenty-six million voted peacefully without a single incident, they voted as Ethiopians and nothing else. We should stand with them and work unremittingly to liberate them from the nefarious TPLF dictatorship.

I am asking young people who are the people of the future not to succumb to views vented by false prophets, and to inform themselves properly and judiciously about the realities in Ethiopia before acting. You must all realize that individually and collectively you are responsible for the fate of millions of people.

When reading the above, some will probably say that I am an old fogey still anchored in the past. With all humility I say that I am not, I have struggled and fought for Human Rights and Democracy in Ethiopia for over half century, much before many of you were born, and I intend to do so until the end. I am a nationalist and patriotic Ethiopian, proud of my country of origin and the people of Ethiopia.

Ethiopia Lezelalem Tenur.

GLOSSARY

Abba	"Father," priestly title
Liqe Papasat Abuna	Metropolitan of the Ethiopian Orthodox Church
Afe-Mesfin	"Mouth of the Duke," spokesperson of the Duke
Afe-Negus	"Mouth of the King," Chief Judicial Magistrate
Ato	"Sir," now "Mr."
Azaj	"Commander"
Balabat	local notable, from a distinguished family
Balambaras	"Commander of the Fortress"
Basha	Rank derived from the Turkish high rank, "Pasha," but considered of lower rank in Ethiopia
Bejirond	"Imperial Treasurer"
Blatta	"Page," the rank of Palace Protocol high officials
Blatten-Geta	"Lord of the Pages" title for Palace Administrators, later honorific
Dejazmach	"Commander of the Gate," Commander of the central body of the armed forces

Emebet-Hoy	"Great Royal Lady" reserved for high ranking women of royal blood.
Fitawrari	"Leader of the Vanguard," nobility title equivalent to Viscount
Hakim	"Doctor"
Iteye	"My sister," equivalent to "Auntie" normally used to address one's aunt or governess
Janhoy Meda	"Field of the Emperor," once Addis Ababa's racecourse
Jantirar	One of the oldest titles in Ethiopia, most often reserved to the male members of the family that ruled over Ambassel, in Wollo
Kegnazmach	"Commander of the Right Wing," military title
Kentiba	"Mayor" or "Lord Mayor"
Kibur	Honorable
Lij	Title issued to sons of the high-ranking nobility
Leul Ras	Title given to heads of cadet branches of the dynasty (the Princes of Tigray, Gojjam, etc.)
Memhir	"Teacher"

Mequanint	The high nobility
Negadras	"Head of the Merchants"
Ras	"Head" nobility title equivalent to Duke
Shalaqa	"Chief of a Thousand," military title equivalent to Major
Tsehafi-Taezaz	"Minister of the Pen," once the most powerful post at the Imperial Court
Woizero	"Dame," nowadays "Mrs."

INDEX